W9-DBZ-107

HARCOURT

SOCIAL Studies

Our Communities

Success for English Learners

Grade 3

Harcourt

SCHOOL PUBLISHERS

www.harcourtschool.com

Printed in the United States of America

ISBN-13: 978-0-15-349407-9
ISBN-10: 0-15-349407-7

4 5 6 7 8 9 10 018 15 14 13 12 11 10 09 08 07

Contents

Introduction

One out of five students in classrooms today speaks a language other than English. When in content area classes, such as social studies, these English language learners are faced with the challenge of learning two aspects of the discipline at the same time. They must learn the specialized language and vocabulary of the content area, including unique grammatical structures, as well as the facts associated with the subject area.

Content area teachers may wonder why an English language learner functions successfully when using conversational English, yet he or she struggles to keep up academically with peers whose first language is English. The fact is that academic English is much more complex and abstract than conversational English. It is very important to understand that this is the normal course of second language development. Research shows that students can acquire high levels of proficiency in conversational English within one or two years. However, to attain proficiency in academic English that is equal to grade-level peers can take much longer.

Success for English Learners provides support for social studies teachers using *Harcourt Social Studies* who have English language learners in their classes. *Harcourt Social Studies* offers English Language Learner notes at point of use in the Teacher Edition. *Success for English Learners* can be used with English language learners who are at the beginning, intermediate, and advanced proficiency levels and who need additional support to be successful with each lesson in *Harcourt Social Studies*.

Challenges for English Learners in Social Studies

Since social studies concepts are abstract, they are particularly language-dependent. In addition, social studies requires prior knowledge that is culture-specific, unlike other subjects. American cultural references that English speakers may recognize automatically will be foreign to English language learners from other countries. The vocabulary and social studies concepts present specific challenges to the English language learner.

The following are examples of vocabulary, grammar, word usage, and syntax challenges that should be considered when planning social studies instruction for English language learners.

SOCIAL STUDIES CHALLENGES	EXAMPLES
Vocabulary	
Abstract concepts	democracy, representation
Specialized vocabulary	monarchy, revolution, liberty
Culture-specific vocabulary	pioneer, frontier, colonists
Sentence Structures	
Embedded clauses	He explored a large area of what was to become the Southeastern United States, including present-day Florida . . .
Unclear references	Would it be difficult for you to move to a new place? What might you like about it?
Unreal past conditions	What might have happened to the colonists on Roanoke Island?
Verb tenses	How might his experiences as a backwoodsman have helped him become a successful leader?
Clauses and factual sequence do not match	This backwoodsman surprised many people when he was elected a Tennessee congressman.
Recognition of Signal Words	
Sequence	First, initially, next, subsequently, after that, then, finally, ultimately
Cause/Effect	As a result, because, consequently, leads to, causes, therefore, in order to, to make
Comparison/Contrast	Like, as, similarly, equally, whereas, on the other hand, unlike, however, although
Rhetorical Patterns	
Generalization/Examples	Their traditional lifestyle has disappeared; they live in modern homes, their food comes from the store, and most communities have television.
Definition/Classification	An island is a landform that is surrounded by water. (Identify class, then add defining characteristics.)
Comparison/Contrast	This is because the land is flat, not hilly and rocky like land in the Northeast.
Time Relationships	"I found Rome a city of bricks and left it a city of marble." Augustus is supposed to have spoken these words as he lay dying. He was Rome's first emperor, and started the first of its great building programs.
Cause/Effect	As president, he doubled the size of the United States when he purchased the Louisiana Territory from France.

© Harcourt

Classroom Strategies for English Learners

We know from research that students learn best when they feel that they are in a safe learning environment. Classroom teachers create that environment in different ways, based on their own unique situations. *Success for English Learners* provides a wide array of instructional suggestions designed to help you help every student experience academic success while reading and learning from *Harcourt Social Studies*. Unit by unit, lesson by lesson, you can find the tools you need to ensure that these important things happen:

- inclusion of and respect for students' cultural backgrounds and life experiences by building bridges to prior knowledge
- accessible, varied vocabulary instruction for all key words
- cognates for appropriate lesson vocabulary
- oral language development through content-based chants
- creative, engaging scaffolding of lessons
- student-generated visuals and graphic organizers that serve as home involvement tools
- sheltered writing experiences

Success for English Learners is designed to help you help students toward their goals: to achieve academic success that is equivalent to their native English speaking classmates.

Identify Proficiency Levels

The ability levels of English learners in any classroom might be similar or mixed. Whatever the situation, the following information is designed to support teachers who have English learners in their classes.

Among English learners, there are many different levels of proficiency. The Proficiency Levels chart shows student traits and research-based "best practices" to help teachers respond appropriately to all student levels. Remember, too, that most English learners comprehend more information than they are able to communicate. The strategies suggested in the Proficiency Levels chart will help teachers reach all learners on any given day.

PROFICIENCY LEVELS

Student Traits	Best Practice
BEGINNING • Students are new to English. • Students respond by pointing, nodding, or using other nonverbal communication, leading to one-word or short-phrase responses. • Students create incomplete meanings from non-print features of text. • Students write very simple texts with many errors.	• Use visuals and real objects as much as possible. • Gesture and dramatize to reinforce meaning. • Provide opportunities for active listening. • Present new vocabulary before each lesson. • Ask only the types of questions which students can respond to nonverbally or verbally (yes, no, list generators, either/or).
INTERMEDIATE • Students understand concepts in concrete contexts. • Students begin to speak in phrases and short sentences. • Students share more freely through spoken and written language. • Students create meaning from text through the use of background knowledge. • Students write using more variety, with fewer errors.	• Keep lessons focused on key concepts; limit details. • Check students' comprehension frequently. • Ask open-ended questions (the five Ws, cloze, descriptions). • Provide corrective feedback on academic language. • Assess students' background knowledge and fill gaps when necessary. • Provide models for students' writing.
ADVANCED • Students join discussions with increased level of grammatical accuracy and language complexity. • Students may still struggle with understanding the language of abstract topics, orally or in text. • Students read and write as ways of learning new information. • Writing is more accurate, with errors that don't affect comprehensibility.	• Encourage students' responses both verbally and in writing. • Challenge students to synthesize information through structural higher-order activities. • Teach and model strategies within a communicative context. • Use graphic organizers to help make the abstract more concrete. • Use guided writing and self- and peer-editing.

Planning and Grouping Strategies

Once English learners' proficiency levels have been determined, that information can be used for a variety of planning purposes, including forming learning groups and tasks. Research suggests that opportunities for English learners to engage in language use within meaningful contexts is essential to developing high levels of language proficiency. Cooperative learning and small-group tasks offer opportunities for focused interaction and for developing meaningful contexts.

Students need to be in mixed groups for many learning tasks, including groups with both English learners and native English speakers. This is important, because a group of learners at similar levels will not be equipped to provide one another the necessary modeling or corrective feedback required for English learning to occur. Beginning students learn from those who are more advanced. More advanced students increase their proficiency when they have leadership roles in groups.

Evidence has shown that carefully designed cooperative learning tasks provided students more practice in speaking and listening than did tasks that were teacher directed. When teachers are planning learning experiences, they should create contextual scenarios that are focused and deliberate in both content-area goals and language goals. The learning task should be highly structured so that students practice using new language skills in a safe environment. Students who are aware of the instructional goals of the task have been shown to make significant gains in learning. Also critical to students' success is corrective feedback regarding students' progress toward those goals. Productive corrective feedback is more than a casual or conversational "recast" of students' speech, writing, spelling and grammatical errors. Teachers must provide explicit feedback about each dimension of language use.

Whether you are pairing students or having them work cooperatively in larger numbers, choose the groupings carefully. Also be sure that the tasks assigned to pairs or groups are purposeful and allow for natural language to flourish.

Reminders for Social Studies Classrooms with English Learners

- **Beware of Tricky Vocabulary** Beyond the high concept load and assumptions of prior knowledge that present challenges for English learners in social studies, several vocabulary issues must be addressed. As in all texts, multiple-meaning words exist in social studies curricula. Additionally, social studies texts present many culture-specific terms *(pioneer, Congress, Gulf Coast)*. Students are most successful when teachers are vigilant about the different usages, both in texts and in the language they use during instruction. Idioms are noticed and explained, as is colloquial language, such as "ace in the hole" or "agree to disagree." Furthermore, once vocabulary is taught, the best teachers work hard to ensure students practice it repeatedly through reading, listening, and in written form.

- **Present Models for All Expected Tasks** Whoever said "A picture is worth a thousand words" could have been speaking directly to teachers of English learners. Making word meanings concrete for English learners is essential when dealing with abstract social studies concepts. Use pictures, gestures, demonstrations, and realia, or real objects. If possible, similarly engage students in acting out concepts or showing their comprehension in ways that are not language dependent.

  For teachers of English learners, another cliché is especially true: "Actions speak louder than words." Instead of using many verbal instructions to explain tasks, show students what you want them to do. Good modeling will result in positive experiences and lower frustration levels for all.

- **Respect All Participation** Remember that the main goal of social studies instruction for English learners is the mastery of academic content and achieving an appropriate level of class participation. The goal is not grammatical perfection, eloquent speech or writing, or error-free interactions. Build a safe, trusting environment where all feel free to contribute. Praise all efforts and tactfully model correct grammar and structures.

Using *Success for English Learners*

The information that follows introduces you to the specific parts of each lesson plan in *Success for English Learners*.

Unit Openers

The Unit Opener lesson plans in this guide are designed to help teachers prepare English learners for the academic language they will encounter throughout the *Harcourt Social Studies* unit. A Reading Focus Skill is taught in the Student Edition and reinforced and practiced at the chapter and lesson levels of *Harcourt Social Studies*.

Success for English Learners provides teachers with a plan for pre-teaching the Reading Focus Skill. Teachers introduce the skill and give several examples that demonstrate it. Vocabulary commonly associated with the skill is defined and made concrete for English learners. Practice-and-apply scenarios suggest appropriate activities for English learners, including using the same graphic organizer featured in the Student Edition of *Harcourt Social Studies*. Having prior experiences with academic language, English learners are now prepared to participate in the *Harcourt Social Studies* lessons.

Compare and Contrast

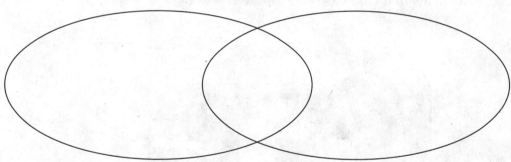

Sequence of Events

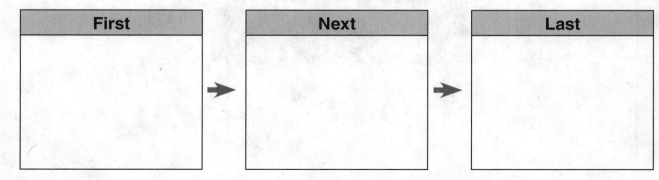

Build Background

Each Lesson Plan begins with Build Background, designed to prepare English learners to study the content of the lesson. **Access Prior Knowledge** helps teachers tap into students' existing knowledge. *Success for English Learners* creates a "common hook" to the students' own experiences about the lesson concepts. When no hook was obvious for a very important concept, a short, simple explanation is provided.

Next, the **Lesson Vocabulary** is introduced. Students are asked to read, write, and define the words in grade-appropriate ways. Engaging vocabulary activities are suggested. Additional program resources are available, including the glossary from the Student Edition of *Harcourt Social Studies* and Word Card blackline masters. In this section, troublesome words from the lesson are called out in the sidebar. These include multiple-meaning words or idiomatic expressions, for example. In addition, cognates are provided. There are many words in Spanish and English that look alike and have almost the same meaning. By listing cognates teachers are able to connect the lesson vocabulary to students' existing knowledge. Teachers can instruct students to add these words to vocabulary notebooks or challenge them to find additional cognates in the lessons.

Then, students are given an opportunity to **Build Fluency.** A chant related to the lesson content provides practice and application of vocabulary and reading skills. Rhythm, rhyme, and repetition are some of the devices used to create fun chants that students will want to repeat over and over.

Scaffolding the Content

Scaffolding the Content is for use during *Harcourt Social Studies* lesson instruction. Critical points of the lesson that English learners should understand are addressed in this section of the Lesson Plan. In **Preview the Lesson,** *Success for English Learners* focuses on key visuals, headings, or other content indicators for students to examine as they scan the text. Vocabulary words taught in Build Background might also be readdressed.

Modify Instruction has suggestions for how to ensure the accessibility and comprehensibility of the content for English learners. The point is to clarify the content and not to simplify it. The Modify Instruction section breaks the lesson content into manageable chunks. The teacher may work directly with small groups of English learners, using the suggestions to bring the content alive and make it more concrete for students.

A critical part of the Lesson Plan is a **blackline master** for students to complete. These pages are designed to help students internalize the main ideas of the lesson. Most often, the page features a graphic organizer that allows students to see concrete connections between ideas. In addition, this page is designed for students to take home and share with family members. A meaningful **School-Home Connection** provides students further opportunities to talk about the social studies content they are learning. In doing so, English learners practice their language skills in a meaningful context.

Suggestions for how to **Extend** the lesson end the Scaffolding the Content section. You will find that these activities review main lesson concepts while giving English learners a new way to synthesize the information.

Apply and Assess

The last part of the lesson plan is called Apply and Assess. It serves two distinct purposes. The Apply section matches the writing or performance activity in the Lesson Review section of the Student Edition. *Success for English Learners* offers sheltered-writing experiences. These activities are designed to help English learners produce a very similar product to that produced by their native-speaking peers.

The Assess section provides a rubric that suggests ways to informally assess students' comprehension of lesson concepts. This rubric includes carefully articulated tasks for students to do. The rubric also gives possible responses expected from students with beginning, intermediate, and advanced language proficiencies.

Conclusion

Throughout the Lesson Plans, *Success for English Learners* has been designed to suggest when to use each section in relation to *Harcourt Social Studies* lesson plans. In addition, estimates are given for how long each section might take. This information is found as a sidebar at point of use in the Lesson Plan.

This guide provides a useful toolbox for teachers to use with English learners in the social studies classroom. From Developing Academic Language to Apply and Assess, *Success for English Learners* is full of strategies and methods that have been proven to increase English learners' language proficiency and their acquisition of content knowledge. Each activity in this guide is designed to help teachers solve students' particular problems or meet a specific need.

When Minutes Count

Success for English Learners is a comprehensive guide for explicit language and content instruction. When time is short, there are some important concepts that can be integrated into lesson plans that will support English language learners. Consider the following ten tips:

For All English Language Learners

1. Provide a low-anxiety environment.

2. Keep your expectations high. Differentiate instructional strategies while teaching the same standards to all students.

Beginning Level

3. Ask questions that can be answered with a single word or by pointing to pictures.

4. Utilize photos, paintings, drawings, and maps as much as possible.

Intermediate Level

5. Frontload vocabulary and language structures.

6. Introduce graphic organizers, and then allow students to use them as a prewriting tool.

7. Use writing frames to scaffold written responses.

Advanced Level

8. Maximize the teachable moments to accelerate the learning of new language forms and to expand vocabulary.

9. Provide ample opportunities to practice, apply, and use language purposefully.

10. Allow students time to reflect on language forms and processes.

Rebecca Valbuena
Language Development Specialist
Stanton Elementary School
Glendora Unified School District

Developing Academic Language

As students explore the topics in this unit, they will be encouraged to compare and contrast different places, people, and ideas. Students will better be able to understand what they read when they recognize the text structures and key words that signal compare-and-contrast relationships.

Introduce Compare and Contrast

Explain to students that when you **compare** two things, you show how they are alike. When you **contrast** two things, you show how they are different. Hold up a pen and a pencil. Draw a Venn diagram on the board. Tell students that this diagram can help them compare and contrast two things that are similar, yet different. In the overlapping section of the diagram, note that both the pen and the pencil are used to write with. In the outer sections, note that pencil marks can be erased, but pen marks cannot. Note any other similarities and differences mentioned by students.

- Before **Compare and Contrast**, p. 4
- 10 minutes

Practice

Write model sentences that show how to talk about the similarities and differences between a pen and a pencil. Have students note words that signal similarities, such as *and* and *too,* and differences, such as *however* and *but*.

I write with a pencil, and I write with a pen, too.
The pencil makes gray marks, but the pen makes blue marks.
I can erase pencil marks. However, I cannot erase pen marks.

Apply

Display the chart below on the board. Read it together. Then have students use a two-column comparison chart like the one below it to note the similarities and differences between Lagos, Nigeria, and Washington, D.C.

Lagos	Washington, D.C.
used to be the capital of Nigeria	is the capital of the United States
near the Gulf of Guinea	next to the Potomac River
not planned to be a capital city	planned to be a capital city
needs more homes for people	needs more homes for people

Lagos		Washington, D.C.
What is different?	What is similar?	What is different?

Build Background

Access Prior Knowledge

Write your town's name on the board, and say it with the class. Ask students to call out people and places that make up this community. Write their ideas on the board. When possible, draw a simple image to illustrate the word. For example, for *house*, write the word *house*, and below it draw a simple house. Circle all the words and images, and explain that all these things make up the town's community.

• Before **Introduce**, p. 14
• 30 minutes

Lesson Vocabulary

Write the word **community** on the board, and say it with the class. Have students say the name of their neighborhood or town in this sentence: _____ *is a community.* Then show students the vocabulary cards, and say each word with them. Point to the people they mentioned during the previous activity, and pair the **citizen** card with the people. Continue to pair the cards with other words and images you've explored on the board. For **business,** students can pair the word with different shops. For **culture,** students can pair the word with a restaurant that serves a culturally specific food. For **law,** students can pair the word with traffic lights or a stop sign. For **government,** students can pair the word with a government official, like a mayor. Your town might not have a **museum,** so you might need to draw a simple rectangular shape to represent a building that people visit. Have students conclude the activity by completing the following sentence with each vocabulary word: *A community has _____.*

Additional Vocabulary Explain these multiple-meaning words and idiomatic phrases, and give examples of how they are used in the book.

Cognates As students read the lesson, you may wish to point out cognates such as: **community/comunidad, culture/cultura, museum/museo.**

behave	order
depend on	ways of life
follow	

Build Fluency

Read aloud the following rhyme, and point out the words that sound alike. Return to the rhyme throughout the lesson to help develop vocabulary, compare-and-contrast skills, and lesson content.

What is a **community?**
A place where people work, live, and play!
What does a community have?
People and places you see every day!
A community has—
  Different **cultures!**
  Businesses, too!
  Laws to follow,
  Governments, too!
Places to learn and
Places to play.
You see your **community**
Every day!

© Harcourt

Scaffolding the Content

Preview the Lesson

Have students study the pictures on pages 14–19. Have them call out words they know that tell about the pictures. Explain what each picture shows.

• During **Teach**, pp. 15–19
• 30 minutes

Modify Instruction

Pass out the activity sheet, and point out that the headings on the chart on the blackline master page are found in the headings of the lesson. Read the headings with the group, then talk about each one.

1 **Many People, One Community** Open your arms to encompass the entire group, and say: *people.* Point to other students in the class, and say: *people.* Help students understand that they are part of their community; a community has people. The people in a community are called *citizens.* On their charts, have students draw themselves and other people that live in their community.

2 **Depending on One Another** Ask a volunteer to help you turn a page or hold up the book, then thank him or her. Explain that the student has helped you. People in a community help each other. They depend on each other. People who have shops and other businesses depend on workers, and on people to buy things. On their charts, have students draw businesses they know in their communities.

3 **Coming Together** Move your arm around the room to indicate the classroom. *You come to school. You learn at school.* Point outside to the playground. *You come to the playground. You play on the playground.* Explain that communities have places where people come together, like schools and playgrounds. On their charts, have students draw pictures of places where they come together.

4 **Following Rules and Laws** Point to rules you have written in the classroom. Have students name other rules they know. Explain that rules and laws keep them safe. People must listen and follow those rules. People who lead a group make the laws. In a community, the people who lead are part of the government. On their charts, have students draw pictures of rules they follow, like stopping at a stop sign.

Extend

Review with students the features of their community that they have drawn and discussed. Then have students compare the images of their community with the images of the community in the book. Have them point to images that are similar, and then have them point to images that are different.

• After **Teach**, pp. 15–19
• 15 minutes

Name _____ Date _____

What Is a Community?

People = Many People, One Community	
Businesses = Depending on One Another	
Play and Learn = Coming Together	
Following Rules and Laws	

 School-Home Connection Invite students to take this chart home to share with their families. Have them explain the pictures they drew and how these pictures relate to their community.

© Harcourt

Apply and Assess

Make a Word Web

Draw a word web on the board with four surrounding circles. In the center circle write: "A Community Has . . . ." Tell students that a community is a place that has people, businesses, places, and laws. Tell students to copy the word web you have started, and ask them to complete the web with a person, a business, a place, and a law they might find in a community. Assist students as necessary. For example:

• During **Close**, p. 19
• 20 minutes

- Beginning students might be able to express their ideas in spoken language but not in written language. Write the words students say on their drawings.

- Intermediate students should be encouraged to write labels and short phrases on their own, or with help from partners.

- Advanced students should be encouraged to write about their pictures in complete sentences.

Informal Lesson Assessment

	Beginning	Intermediate	Advanced
Task	Student draws a person, business, place, and rule that a community has. Student dictates one-word labels for their pictures.	Student draws and writes labels or short phrases that tell about a person, business, place, and law in a community.	Student draws and writes sentences that tell about a person, business, place, and law in a community.
Below Expectations	• drawings do not represent the people, businesses, places, or rules in a community • student is unable to verbalize ideas	• label or phrase does not correspond with the picture • spelling is invented	• sentence corresponds to the picture, but the spelling is invented
Meets Expectations	• drawings represent a person, business, place, and rule in a community • student is able to dictate labels for parts of the community	• label or phrase corresponds with drawing • spelling is approximate	• sentence corresponds to the picture, and the spelling is correct • sentence construction is slightly wrong
Above Expectations	• drawings represent a person, business, place, and rule in a community • student is able to write some labels on his or her own	• label or phrase corresponds with drawing • spelling is correct	• sentence corresponds to the picture, and the spelling is correct • sentence construction is complete and correct

Build Background

Access Prior Knowledge

Have students tell what they learned about communities in the previous lesson. Discuss the things that make a community and the things that a community has. Write these things on the board. Then ask students if they think all communities are the same. Point to the words on the board, and say: *Do all communities have the same businesses? The same laws?*

- Before **Introduce**, p. 20
- 30 minutes

Lesson Vocabulary

Have students look outside the window. Ask: *What is it like outside?* Suggest words to describe the weather, for example, *Is it sunny? Cold? Warm? Windy?* Use hand motions or pantomimes to relay meaning. Then write the word *weather* on the board, and point to the outside. Write the word **climate** on the board next to *weather*, and say: *Climate is weather over a long time. Different communities have different climates.* Show the pictures on page 20. Ask students to finger-trace each place to "feel" the differences. Motion your hand around to encompass all the pictures, and say the word **landforms**. Write *landforms* on the board. Point to the desert photograph, and say: *This is a desert.* Let students describe it. Then hold up a book, a pencil, and some paper. Say: *I buy these things. Things people buy are called* **goods**. Write *goods* on the board. Then point to yourself, and say: *I am a teacher. I teach. Teaching is a service. A job a person does for you is a service.*

Additional Vocabulary Write the word *Earth* on the board. Run your finger below it, and have students say it with you. Then display your classroom globe, or a wall map that shows the entire Earth. Say: *This is Earth. We live on Earth. We live in communities on Earth.* Point to names of cities and towns, and say: *These are communities on Earth.*

Cognates As students read the lesson, you may wish to point out cognates such as: **climate/clima, desert/desierto, services/servicios, history/historia, geography/geografía.**

bodies of water
built around
Earth
events
history
location
mountains

Build Fluency

Read aloud the following rhyme, and point out the words that sound alike. Return to the rhyme throughout the lesson to help develop vocabulary, compare-and-contrast skills, and lesson content.

Communities are not the same.
How many differences can you name?
Climate is different from place to place.
Landforms give each a different face.
Jobs and businesses may not be the same,
And the history of each can also change.
Goods are items that you buy,
Like food and clothes and toys to try.
People do **services** for me and you,
Communities have differences—these are a few!

© Harcourt

Scaffolding the Content

Preview the Lesson

• During **Teach**, pp. 20–25
• 30 minutes

Some students might not understand the meaning of the word *different*. Hold up two objects that are the same, like two pencils, and say: *Same*. Then hold up a pencil and a crayon, and say: *Different*. Repeat the activity with other same-and-different objects so students become comfortable with the idea. Another example might be two sheets of notebook paper (same); notebook paper and construction paper (different).

Then say: *Communities are different*. Look through the photographs in the lesson, and have students point out how they are different. Have them say sentences such as: *This community has _____, This community looks like _____, This community does not have _____, This community does not look like _____*. Then explain that students are going to learn how communities are different from each other.

Modify Instruction

Draw a large Venn diagram on the board, and explain its function. Point to the middle circle, and say: *Same*. Point to the outer circles, and say: *Different*. Then pass out one blackline master page to each student, and make sure they recognize the diagram as the one you have drawn on the board. Begin exploring the chapter with the group.

1 Point to the word *geography* in the first heading, and have students write this word in the center circle of their Venn diagrams. Say: *All communities have geography. Geography is climate and landforms. Communities have different geography.* Have students write *climate* and *landforms* in the center circle. Then have students draw one place that has a different climate or landform in the first outer circle, and another place with a different climate and landform in the second outer circle, based on the photos in the lesson.

2 Pass out a second Venn diagram, and have students write *history* in the center circle. Say: *All communities have history. Communities have different history.* Have students write *Greenbelt, Maryland = new* in one outer circle, and *Clarksville, Indiana = old* in another outer circle. Say: *Greenbelt is a new community. It has been a community for a short time. Clarksville is an old community. It has been a community for a long time.*

3 Pass out a final Venn diagram, and have students write *jobs* in the center circle. Say: *All communities have jobs. Communities have different jobs.* Then invite students to draw two different jobs in the outer circles for two different communities in the lesson.

Extend

• After **Teach**, pp. 20–25
• 20 minutes

Ask students to draw a picture of their own community or a made-up community. Tell them to include the climate, a landform, something that tells about the community's history, and a business (goods and services) that it offers. Then have students create their own Venn diagrams to compare and contrast each other's communities.

© Harcourt

Success for English Learners ▪ 7

How Communities Are Alike and Different

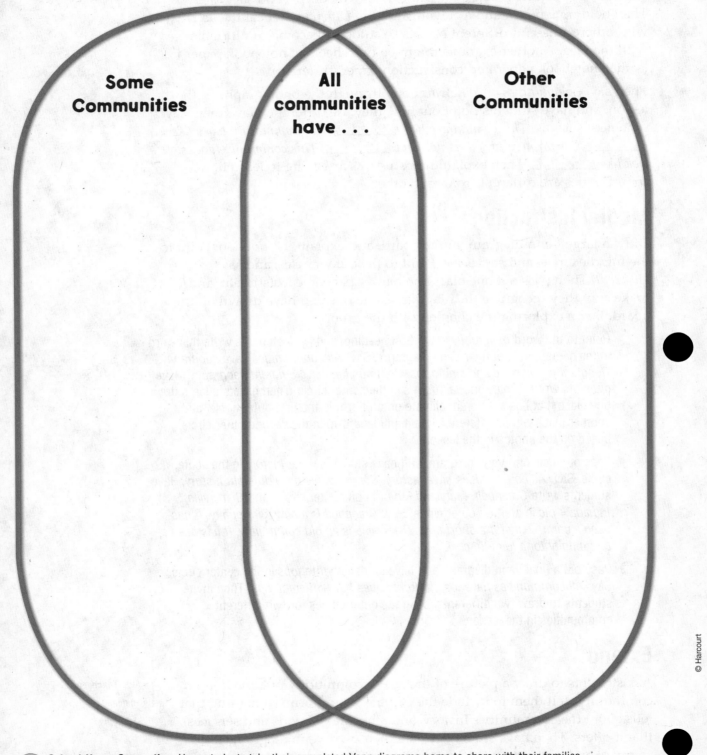

Some Communities

All communities have . . .

Other Communities

🚌 **School-Home Connection** Have students take their completed Venn diagrams home to share with their families. Ask them to explain what *geography, history,* and *jobs* mean and how they relate to communities, using their Venn diagrams to guide them.

© Harcourt

Apply and Assess

Write a Description

On the board, write the words *Our Community*. Then write the key points from the lesson on the board: *geography, history, jobs.* Ask students to draw pictures and/or write descriptions that tell about their community's geography, history, and jobs. Because some students may be new to the community, elicit what they know, and then share new information that will help them complete the activity. If possible, display pictures of your community to help them recall places and features from which to build their own ideas. Provide assistance as needed. For example:

• During **Close**, p. 25
• 20 minutes

- Beginning students can dictate their ideas or labels as you write them on their drawings.
- Intermediate students should be encouraged to write labels and short phrases for their drawings themselves.
- Advanced students should be encouraged to write about their pictures in complete sentences.

Informal Lesson Assessment

	Beginning	Intermediate	Advanced
Task	Students draw and label pictures that show the geography, history, and jobs in their community.	Students draw and write labels or short phrases to show the geography, history, and jobs in their community.	Students draw pictures and write complete sentences that describe the geography, history, and jobs in their community.
Below Expectations	• drawings do not represent the community • student is unable to verbally express ideas about the community	• labels or phrases do not correspond with the pictures of the community • spelling is invented	• sentences correspond to the pictures, but the spelling is invented
Meets Expectations	• drawing represents the community • student is able to say or write key words that tell about the community	• labels or phrases correspond with the drawings • spelling is approximate	• sentences correspond to the pictures, and the spelling is correct • sentence construction is slightly wrong
Above Expectations	• drawing represents the community • student is able to talk or write about the community in coherent sentences	• labels or phrases correspond with the drawings • spelling is correct	• sentences correspond to the pictures, and the spelling is correct • sentence construction is complete and correct

© Harcourt

Build Background

Access Prior Knowledge

Ask students: *Where do we live?* Have students say with you: *We live in _____.* Then say: *My aunt lives in a* different *community. She lives in _____.* Pantomime talking on the phone, and say: *I use the telephone to talk to my aunt.* Pantomime writing a letter, and say: *I write letters to my aunt, too.* Ask students to tell (or pantomime) how they "talk" to friends and families in other communities.

- Before **Introduce**, p. 26
- 30 minutes

Lesson Vocabulary

Have volunteers act out talking, writing a letter, and using the telephone, and write each word/phrase on the board. Have the class repeat the actions as they say the words. Then draw a circle around these words, draw an arrow pointing to another circle, and within the second circle write the word **communication.** Say: *Talking, writing letters, and using the telephone are kinds of* communication. Indicate your class computer, or show students a picture of a computer, and have them say *computer* with you. Pantomime typing, and ask: *Can you also use the computer to communicate?* Elicit students' responses. Say: *You can send a letter with the computer. When you send a letter with the computer, you call it e-mail. You send letters using the* **Internet.** *The Internet is on your computer.* Say: *United States* as you write it on the board. Have students name other countries they know. Draw a large circle around all the countries, draw an arrow pointing to another circle, and within the second circle write the word **nation.** Say: *All these places are* nations. *Communities are parts of nations.*

Additional Vocabulary The idiom *stay in touch* might confuse students. Say the word *touch,* and touch things near you. Then say: *To stay in touch means to communicate with people in different communities.* Continue introducing other words and phrases listed in the margin, having students use them in sentences wherever possible.

Cognates As students read the lesson, you may wish to point out cognates such as: **communication/comunicación, connection/conexión, information/información, nation/nación, telephone/teléfono.**

e-mail

forms (of communication)

leaders

live pictures

share

stay connected

stay in touch

supplies

ways of life

Build Fluency

Read aloud the following rhyme, and point out the words that sound alike. Return to the rhyme throughout the lesson to help develop vocabulary, compare-and-contrast skills, and lesson content.

Communities talk through **communication.**
Telephones, letters, visiting much,
Help people communicate and stay in touch.
The computer and the **Internet** can help us, too,
To all stay connected—me and you!

© Harcourt

Scaffolding the Content

Preview the Lesson

On the board, draw a circle, and write the name of your community within it. Then have students offer the names of other communities. Write these names on the board within circles too, scattered around the circle with your community's name. Point to each community name and say: *This is a community.* Then draw a wavy line from each circle to your community circle. Say: *These communities are now connected!*

• During **Teach**, pp. 27–29
• 30 minutes

To further get across the idea of connected communities, give each student a long piece of yarn. With the yarn dangling, tell students that they are *not* connected. Then have students each hold an end of another classmate's yarn while holding their own, and say: *Now you are connected!* Explain that letters, telephones, and computers connect communities.

Modify Instruction

Point out the United States on a wall map or globe. Then point out other countries, such as Canada and Mexico. Pointing to a border town in Texas, trace a line to the closest town in Mexico, and say: *These communities are close.* Then choose a community in the northern United States and trace a line to the same town in Mexico. Say: *These communities are far.* Then say: *These communities can all communicate. Communication connects these communities.* Explore how in more detail.

1 **Communities Are Everywhere** As students watch, you will recreate the diagram from the blackline master page. Pass out a copy to each student. Start by drawing a rectangle at the top of the board and writing in *The United States.* Have students do so as well. Say: *The United States is a nation.*

2 **Community Connections** In the diamond-shaped box, have students read the word *communication.* Encourage them to draw the ways in which people can communicate, or stay in touch, as discussed on page 27. Students should draw computers, letters, and the telephone. Have them label each drawing and include *Internet* with *computer.*

3 **Sister Cities** Move on to "Sister Cities," and have students write the community *St. Louis, Missouri* in the top left circle. Have them write the community *Bogor* in the bottom left circle, and then *Indonesia* in the bottom rectangle. Say: *Bogor is a community. Indonesia is a nation. Bogor and St. Louis are like sisters. They help each other.*

4 **Helping Each Other** Have students finger-trace from the *community* circle along the wavy lines to *communication* circle and the next *community* circle. Say: *These communities are far away. These communities are still connected.* Have students explain, or point to pictures that show how the communities are connected.

Extend

Have students write the name of their community in the top right circle and then the name of another community and nation in the bottom right of the diagram. Have them discuss how their community could be connected to this other community.

• After **Teach**, pp. 27–29
• 10 minutes

© Harcourt

Name _____ Date _____

DIRECTIONS Listen to your teacher. Fill in the spaces to show how communities in different nations can talk to each other. The bottom two circles are for your own community and a community you would like to be connected to.

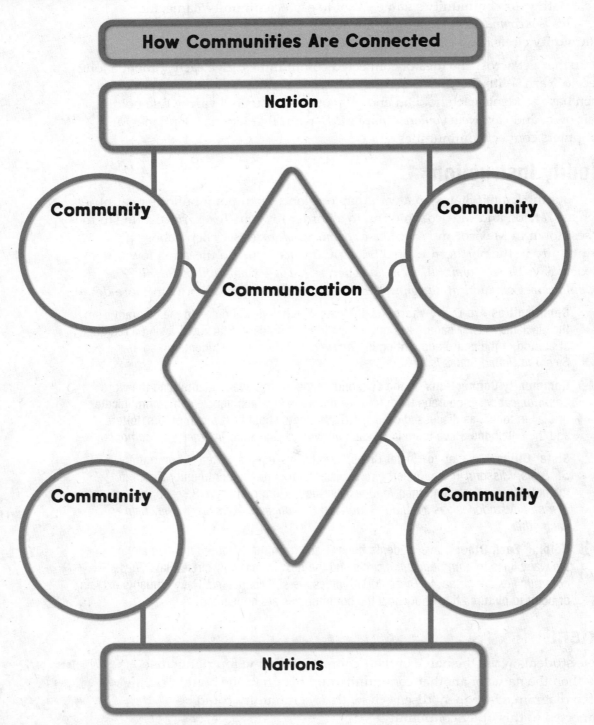

How Communities Are Connected

Nation

Community

Community

Communication

Community

Community

Nations

 School-Home Connection Tell students to take their diagrams home. Have them find examples in their homes that show how they communicate, or stay in touch with people in other communities, such as letters they have written, the computer, e-mail, and the telephone.

© Harcourt

Apply and Assess

Write an E-mail

• During **Close**, p. 29
• 20 minutes

Students might need an example of an e-mail, or any letter, in order to get started. Provide samples of letters, either from your own collections, from letters other students have written, or from other texts. Hold up the letters, and say: *Letters keep us connected. Letters are communication.* Point out the parts of the letter, and then tell students that you would like to have them write letters to a family member or friend in another community. Ask them to think about something they would like to tell about their community in their letters. Assist students as needed. For example:

- Allow beginning students to draw pictures to show their ideas and to tell you what they have drawn as you write down their words.

- Encourage intermediate students to help each other form ideas in both pictures and phrases, or short sentences.

- Challenge advanced students to write an e-mail without pictures, if possible, and to write in complete sentences.

Informal Lesson Assessment

	Beginning	Intermediate	Advanced
Task	Students draw and label pictures to convey how a person communicates with a person in a different community.	Students draw and write phrases or short sentences to convey how a person communicates with a person in a different community.	Students write sentences about how a person communicates with a person in a different community.
Below Expectations	• drawings do not represent forms of communication • student is unable to verbally express ideas about communication	• phrases or short sentences do not correspond with the picture • spelling is invented	• sentences are incomplete • spelling is invented • sentences do not convey information about communication
Meets Expectations	• drawing represents communication • spoken or written words correspond with the drawings	• phrases or short sentences correspond with the drawings • spelling is approximate	• sentences are complete • sentence construction is slightly wrong • sentences convey information about communication
Above Expectations	• drawing represents communication • student is able to talk or write about communication in phrases or sentences	• phrases or short sentences correspond with the drawings • spelling is correct	• sentence construction and spelling is correct • sentences convey specific details about communication

© Harcourt

Build Background

Access Prior Knowledge

Ask students what they know about their community. You might list their ideas in the first column of a K-W-L chart—*What I Know.* Show students how much they know by asking questions, such as: *What is the climate like? What history do you know? What businesses does our community have?*

• Before **Introduce**, p. 32
• 30 minutes

Lesson Vocabulary

Ask students to brainstorm ways to learn more about communities. Draw a word web on the board, and in the center circle, write: *How I Can Learn About My Community?* Then talk with students about places to find information. Write each place in the outer circle of the web. Write the phrase **reference work** in one circle. Hold up several reference books that you have handy. Ask: *Are these books reference works or comic books?* Say: *Reference works have information.* List these works within the circle. Write the word **ancestor** in another circle. Explain that an ancestor is someone from your family who lived a long time ago; a person's family history is his or her **heritage.** Write *family* and *heritage* in the circle. In another circle, write **historic site.** Explain that a *site* is a *place.* A *historic site* is a place where something important in history happened. Finally, write ***historical society*** in a circle. Explain that a *society* is a group of people. A *historical society* is a group of people who are interested in history.

Additional Vocabulary Introduce all the vocabulary listed in the margin. Have students use the words in sentences.

Cognates As students read the lesson, you may wish to point out cognates such as: **detect/detectar, family/familia, historical/histórico, organization/organización, photograph/fotografía, reference/referencia, society/sociedad.**

clues	interview
cultures	past
detective	search
discover	set of values

Build Fluency

Read aloud the following rhyme, and point out the words that sound alike. Return to the rhyme throughout the lesson to help develop vocabulary, compare-and-contrast skills, and lesson content.

Your community is a special place,
There is so much to know.
You want to learn more about this place.
Where, then, can you go?
Libraries have **reference works,**
Like photographs and maps.
An interview with someone you know
Can tell you about the past.
Historic sites are also good
To learn about long ago.

© Harcourt

Scaffolding the Content

Preview the Lesson

Talk about the idea of students as detectives. Say: *We are detectives. Detectives find information. How can we find information about a community?* Tell students they will fill in the K part of the K-W-L chart. Pass the magnifying glass to students, and let them say these words with you. Encourage students to relate the photos to learning about their community:

• During **Teach**, pp. 33–37
• 30 minutes

Page 33: *I am a detective. I can learn about my community. I can read books to learn about my community.*

Page 34: *I am a detective. I can learn about my community. I can talk to, or interview, people to learn about my community.*

Page 36: *I am a detective. I can learn about my community. I can visit special places to learn about my community.*

Modify Instruction

Tell students that to learn about their community they can follow some steps, or a process. Pass out three copies of the blackline master page to each student, and point to the numbered boxes and the arrows. Explain that the arrows lead to the next step in the process. Then work through each section of the lesson.

❶ **Become a Detective** Read the heading on the blackline master page, and then have students read the heading in the text: *Become a Detective.* Have students write this heading on the first line of the first activity sheet. Write the word *library* on the board, and have students find it in the text. Explain that a library is a place to find information. Have students write *library* in the first box on the flow chart. Say that the next step is to find *reference works* at the library; have students find *reference works* in the text and write it in the second box on their charts. Then tell students that the third step is to look at reference works like maps and photographs. Write these words on the board, and have students write them in the third box on the blackline master page.

❷ **Interview Someone in Your Community** Continue in this manner with the lesson heading *Interview Someone in Your Community.* Tell students that the first step in an interview is to find someone to ask, like a business owner. The second step is to write the questions. The third step is to ask the questions. Students can also complete another flow chart with *family members*, *ancestors*, and *heritage*.

❸ **Write to or Visit Special Places** For the final blackline master page, have students write *Write to or Visit Special Places* at the top. Have them write *historic site* or *historical society* in the first box; *history information* in the second box; and *photographs*, *books*, *maps*, *diaries*, and *newspapers* in the last box.

Extend

Review with students the first column of the K-W-L chart from "Access Prior Knowledge." Ask students what questions they have about their communities, and tell them to write their questions in the second column of the chart: *What I Want to Know.* Then have students list places to find this information in the third column and title it *Where to Find Information.*

• After **Teach**, pp. 33–37
• 20 minutes

© Harcourt

Name _____ Date _____

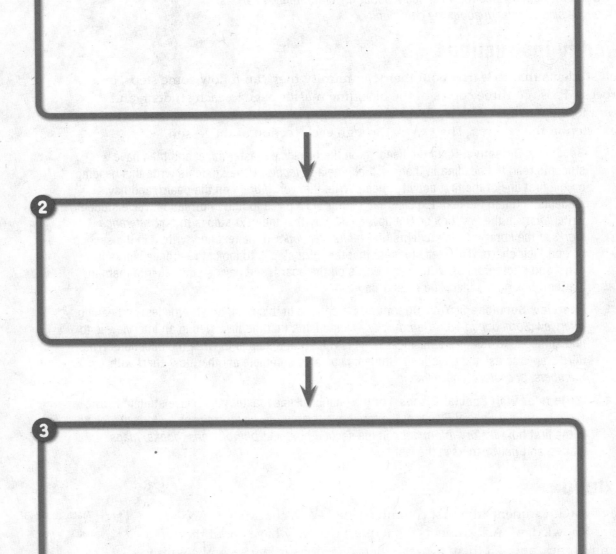

How to Learn About Our Community

Title: _____

1

2

3

 School-Home Connection Tell students to take their completed flow charts home. Have them explain to their families that they are detectives, learning about their community. Suggest that students interview someone in their families to learn new information about the community.

Apply and Assess

Make a Web Page

Write the term *web page* on the board, and say it for the group. Have
students share what they know about web pages. Ideally, print several web
pages from a child-oriented web site to share with the group. Explain that
a web page is what you see on a computer screen when you use the Internet.
Web pages tell information. Say that you would like students to make a web
page to tell where they can find information about a community. Pass out
large drawing paper, and tell students to make their web pages with both
pictures and words. Guide students as necessary, for example:

• During **Close**, p. 37
• 20 minutes

- Beginning students can dictate their ideas as you write them on their drawings.
- Intermediate students should be encouraged to write short phrases that tell about
  the drawings on their web pages.
- Advanced students should be encouraged to write in complete and interesting
  sentences.

Informal Lesson Assessment

	Beginning	Intermediate	Advanced
Task	Students draw and label pictures that show places where they could find information about their community.	Students draw pictures of places to find information about their community and write short labels.	Students write complete sentences describing places to find information about their community.
Below Expectations	• drawings do not show places to find information • labels do not correspond to pictures • student is unable to verbally express ideas	• phrases do not correspond with the pictures • spelling is invented	• sentences do not tell where to find information • sentences are written incorrectly
Meets Expectations	• drawings represent places to find information • student is able to say key words	• labels or phrases correspond with the illustrations • spelling is approximate	• sentences tell how to find information • sentence construction is slightly wrong
Above Expectations	• drawings represent places to find information • student is able to talk about the places in coherent sentences	• labels or phrases correspond with the illustrations • spelling is correct	• sentences tell how to find information • sentences are correct

© Harcourt

Build Background

Access Prior Knowledge

Ask students to think about things that a community has. Start a chart on the board, and list their ideas. Then ask students if they think their community is a big community or a small community. Use your arms to indicate *big* and *small*. Encourage students to explain their ideas.

• Before **Introduce**, p. 42
• 30 minutes

Lesson Vocabulary

Show students a picture of a city, like the one on page 42. Point to the picture, and say *city*, and have students repeat the word. Explain that a city is the biggest kind of community. Point to the list students generated in "Access Prior Knowledge," and have students repeat with you as you write the word *many* before each item on the list: *many people, many buildings, many businesses*, and so on. Then insert the word *urban* into the list title: *An **urban** community has _____*. Point to the word *people* on the list, and explain that all the people who live in a place are a *population.* Then act out different ways of getting somewhere, such as driving a car. Have students draw simple pictures on the board. Circle all the pictures, and label them *transportation.* Show students the picture on page 45. Point out the boats and the buildings. Explain that a place where boats stop is a **harbor.** Then point to different areas of the country on a United States map. Explain that each area is a **region** of the United States.

Additional Vocabulary Introduce all the vocabulary listed in the margin.

Cognates As students read the lesson, you may wish to point out cognates such as: **apartment/apartamento, region/región, transportation/transporte, urban/urbano,-a.**

allows	lies
catch (the bus)	rides (the subway)
close by	skyscraper
district	subway
downtown	waterfront

Build Fluency

Read aloud the following rhyme, and point out the words that sound alike. Return to the rhyme throughout the lesson to help develop vocabulary, compare-and-contrast skills, and lesson content.

You say you like a lot of people,
    Jobs, and buildings, too.
Then you must go see a city—
    It's the place for you!
A city is an **urban** place.
    They're on every coast.
Their **population** is always large:
    New York City has the most.
A city has so many people
    And different things to do.
Ride the bus or ride the train—
    There's **transportation,** too!

© Harcourt

Scaffolding the Content

Preview the Lesson

Tell students that they are going to take a pretend trip. They will be traveling to a city in the United States called Baltimore. Write *Baltimore* on the board, and have students say it with you. Pull down your classroom wall map, or spread out a map of the United States on a table. Show students their community on the map. Then trace a finger from your community to the region in which Baltimore is found (the mid-Atlantic). Encourage students to find the word *Baltimore* before you get there.

• During **Teach**, pp. 43–47
• 30 minutes

Remind students that Baltimore is an urban community. Ask: *What do you think we will see in Baltimore?* List their ideas, for example: *many people, tall buildings, many businesses, a harbor, transportation.* Return to the list as students "visit" Baltimore in the chapter.

Modify Instruction

Tell students that you are going to give them a checklist (the blackline master page). It will list things that they will see in a city. As they visit Baltimore and other cities in the lesson, they should check off what they see.

1 **Communities Large and Small** Ask students to look at the first column of their charts, and have them draw pictures for each thing an urban community has—many people, tall buildings, many businesses, a harbor, and transportation. Point to the phrases *many people, tall buildings,* and *businesses* in the lesson.

2 **Baltimore, an Urban Community** Now tell students that they will visit the urban community of Baltimore! Explain that a girl who lives in Baltimore will show them around. Her name is Kelsey. Have students find the words *Baltimore* and *Kelsey* in the lesson. As students explore Baltimore, tell them to look for the things on their lists that an urban community has. As you come across each item, have students write a check mark in the box on the list.

3 **Other Urban Communities** Ask students if they enjoyed visiting Baltimore and having Kelsey as a guide. Explain that now they are going to visit other urban communities in the United States. Tell students that you will be their guide this time. The first stop is New York City. Have students listen as you read the text. Tell them to listen for the things that a city has—many people, tall buildings, many businesses, a harbor, and transportation. Tell students to check off these things on their lists, and then review to make sure they have understood. Continue in this way, acting as a guide as students visit Chicago and then Los Angeles.

Extend

Review with students the things that an urban community has. Then have students use the checklist to see if their community is a city. Have them draw their own checklist on the back of the activity sheet, and go over each point with them. Does their community have a lot of people? Tall buildings? Many businesses? A harbor? Different transportation? Have students explain their ideas and conclusions.

• After **Teach**, pp. 43–47
• 15 minutes

Name _____ Date _____

DIRECTIONS Draw pictures to show what you will see in an urban community. Check off the things that are in each urban community you visit.

Urban Communities

An Urban Community Has:	Baltimore	New York City	Chicago	Los Angeles
Many people				
Tall buildings				
Many businesses				
A harbor				
Transportation				

 School-Home Connection Tell students to share their charts with their families. Then have students create a word web with their families, with "Urban Communities" in the center circle. In the outer circles, have students write the names of cities from this lesson and any other cities their families know.

© Harcourt

Apply and Assess

Create a Postcard

Not all students may be familiar with a postcard format. If possible, bring in samples of postcards to pass around the group. If not, hold up a sheet of paper, and say: *A postcard has a picture on one side.* Turn the paper over and say: *A postcard has space to write on the other side.* Then pass out drawing paper on which students can create their postcards. On one side, ask them to draw a picture that shows an urban community. Let them use pictures in the chapter as models. On the other side, ask them to write what makes an urban community special.

- During **Close**, p. 47
- 20 minutes

- Beginning students can dictate words as you write them on the blank side of the postcard.
- Intermediate students should be encouraged to write words or phrases on their own, or with the aid of partners.
- Advanced students should be encouraged tell about an urban community in complete sentences.

Informal Lesson Assessment

	Beginning	Intermediate	Advanced
Task	Student draws an urban community and says words that tell about it.	Student draws an urban community and then writes words or phrases that tell about it.	Student draws an urban community and then writes complete sentences that tell about it.
Below Expectations	• drawing does not show an urban community • student is unable to say words that tell about a city	• labels or phrases do not tell about an urban community • spelling is invented	• sentences are incomplete and do not convey information about a city • sentences are written incorrectly
Meets Expectations	• drawing represents an urban community • student is able to say key words about a city	• labels or phrases tell about an urban community • spelling is approximate	• sentences are complete and tell about a city • sentence construction is slightly wrong
Above Expectations	• drawing represents an urban community • student is able to express ideas about a city in more complete thoughts	• labels or phrases tell about an urban community • spelling is correct	• sentences are complete and tell about a city • sentences are correct • sentences are interesting

Build Background

Access Prior Knowledge

Have students review what they have learned about a city or an urban community. Have them show the size of various cities, using their arms to indicate *large* and *small*. Then have students hold their arms as if they are holding a giant ball, and ask them to explain all the things they would find in a city. As students watch, make a smaller circle with your arms, and ask students if a community can be smaller than a city. Let them share ideas.

• Before **Introduce**, p. 52
• 30 minutes

Lesson Vocabulary

Write the word *urban* on the board, and have students read it with you. Then write the letters *sub* in front of *urban*, creating the word **suburban.** With your arms, make the small circle again, and ask students to make the circle, too. Say: *A suburban community is smaller than an urban community.* As students watch, erase the letters *an*, and read the new word with them: **suburb.** Say: *A suburb is a suburban community. A city is an urban community.* Have students say the sentences with you. You might also write these word equations on the board to help students make the connection: *suburb = suburban community; city = urban community.*

Additional Vocabulary In order to understand the difference between a suburb and a city, students need to know words to help them make this comparison. Through hand motions, help students understand these words as they say sentences that connect to the topic. For example: *Near: A suburb is* near *a city. Smaller: A suburb is* smaller *than a city. Space: A suburb has more* space *than a city. States: A suburb can be in different* states *around a city.* The idiom *heading to* might also give students problems. Teach the remaining words at right, using the words in the context of the lesson.

as more and more . . .
compete
edge
heading to
its own
near
offer
smaller
space
states

Cognates As students read the lesson, you may wish to point out cognates such as: **compete/competir, connect/conectar, park/parque, states/estados, station/estación, supermarket/supermercado, theater/teatro, train/tren.**

Build Fluency

Read aloud the following rhyme, and point out the words that sound alike. Return to the rhyme throughout the lesson to help develop vocabulary, compare-and-contrast skills, and lesson content.

Leave the buildings! Leave the city!
What do you find? Another community!
You find a **suburb**, a different place.
A **suburban** community, with more open space.
Fewer people live here, that is true.
But it's still a great place with lots to do!
So if the city is not for you,
Try a suburb! It's a community, too!

© Harcourt

Scaffolding the Content

Preview the Lesson

Point out the size of your desk, and say: *large*. Then point out a student's desk, and say: *smaller*. Tell them to imagine that your desk is a large city and their desks are the smaller suburbs. Let students stand up and walk among the "city and suburbs," and ask them what they notice. For example: *A suburb is smaller than a city. A suburb is outside a city. There is one city, but many suburbs.* Share with students that as they explore this lesson, they will learn more about how a suburban community is similar to and different from an urban community.

• During **Teach**, pp. 53–55
• 30 minutes

Modify Instruction

Have students sit at their desks, reminding them that they are "suburbs." Then hand out the blackline master page, and tell students that they will fill it out to compare how a suburban community and an urban community are similar and different.

1. **Maplewood, A Suburban Community** Read the heading in the lesson with the class, and then have students match the heading in the top box of their charts. Point out that the top box is a bit smaller than the bottom box, and let students guess why (a suburb is smaller than a city). Then tell students that a boy named John is going to tell them about the suburb of Maplewood. Have students draw pictures or write key words in the Maplewood box to tell about it, for example: *houses, tree-lined streets, small stores, shopping centers, parks, movie theater, supermarket, school.*

2. **Urban Connections** Have students trace their fingers along the lines that lead from the Maplewood box to the New York City box. Ask students what these lines might mean, and say that the lines show that Maplewood and New York City are connected. Have students write *roads and cars, trains,* and *subways* on each line to show the ways that people go to and from the suburbs and the city. To further develop the concept, roll out mural paper between students' desks (the suburbs) and your desk (the city), and have students "travel" between the suburbs and the city.

3. In the bottom box of the chart, have students write the things that people enjoy in a city that they might not find in the suburbs, as listed in the lesson, such as theaters, museums, cultural attractions, and perhaps even sports arenas.

4. Finally, add one or two desks to your suburbs. Ask students why a suburb might grow, and agree that people and businesses continue to move there.

Extend

Let students role-play living in a suburb and visiting a city. As they sit at their desks (a suburb), have each student tell about something he or she might do in a city. Then have the student get up, "travel" along the mural paper to the city, and repeat what he or she could do here. Prompt beginning students as needed, but encourage intermediate and advanced students to express ideas on their own and more fully.

• After **Teach**, pp. 53–55
• 20 minutes

© Harcourt

Name _____ Date _____

DIRECTIONS Tell about a suburban community in the top box. Write how a suburban community connects to an urban community on the lines. Then write about an urban community in the bottom box.

A Suburban Community

Maplewood, a Suburban Community

New York City, an Urban Community

 School-Home Connection Ask students to take their activity sheets home to share with their families. Tell students to talk with their families about the things they might like to do in a city or in a suburb. Have students trace the lines that lead between the urban and suburban activities.

© Harcourt

Apply and Assess

Make a Flyer

• During **Close**, p. 55
• 20 minutes

The word *flyer* might be confusing to some students, because they might mistake it for a person who flies an airplane (spelled *flier*). Praise students for knowing this word, but then explain that *flyer* has another meaning. Show an advertising flyer from a newspaper, or one that your school prints to tell about field trips or other activities. Have students tell you the purpose of this item. Say that a flyer is something that tells people about a place or an event through pictures and a few words. Invite students to make flyers to tell about a general suburban community.

- Beginning students can draw pictures and dictate their ideas as you write them on their flyers.

- Intermediate students should be encouraged to write labels and short phrases to tell about their drawings.

- Advanced students should be encouraged to tell about a suburban community in complete sentences that accompany their drawings.

Informal Lesson Assessment

	Beginning	Intermediate	Advanced
Task	Students answer *yes/no* questions about suburban communities, such as *Are suburban communities bigger than urban communities? Are suburban communities connected to urban communities?*	Ask students to use short phrases to describe suburban communities.	Ask students to write a short paragraph to describe suburban communities.
Below Expectations	• all or most questions answered incorrectly • no answers given	• few or no phrases given, or phrases are incomprehensible • two to four phrases, but none are correct	• no correct reasons or regions are given • no complete sentences • many errors
Meets Expectations	• half the questions answered correctly	• two to four comprehensible phrases • most are correct	• some correct reasons and regions are given • most complete sentences • a few errors
Above Expectations	• all answers are correct	• more than four comprehensible phrases • all are correct	• sentences adequately describe a suburb • sentences are correct • sentences are interesting

Build Background

Access Prior Knowledge

Review with students what they have learned about urban and suburban communities. Write *urban community* on the board, and ask students to draw a simple picture that shows an urban community. Repeat the exercise with *suburban community*. Have students tell how communities can be different sizes, from very big to small. Ask students if they think a community can be even smaller than a suburb, and encourage students to share ideas.

• Before **Introduce**, p. 56
• 30 minutes

Lesson Vocabulary

Draw an arrow connecting *urban community* to *suburban community*. Then draw an arrow moving away from *suburban community*, and write *rural community*. Explain that a **rural** community is a place that is smaller and farther away from a city than a suburb. Write the word **agriculture** on the board, and display for students some fruits and vegetables (or pictures of them). Say: *Agriculture means growing foods*. Then invite a volunteer to role-play buying and selling the fruits and vegetables with you. Say: *An economy means making and buying and selling things*.

Additional Vocabulary The use of the word *country* and *countryside* might be confusing to students, because the word *country* is used in two very different ways. Throughout much of the textbook, *country* refers to a nation. However, in *countryside* on pages 56 and 57, *country* refers to a rural area. Write the word *country* on the board, and explain that it can have two meanings. Write: *country = nation* and *country = rural area*. Preview the use of each word at right in the context of the lesson.

Cognates As students read the lesson, you may wish to point out cognates such as: **agriculture/agricultura, center/centro, complex/complejo, economy/economía, hospital/hospital, restaurant/restaurante, rural/rural, university/universidad.**

community center
country
countryside
county fair
crops
discount store
make up
soccer complex
woods

Build Fluency

Read aloud the following rhyme, and point out the words that sound alike. Return to the rhyme throughout the lesson to help develop vocabulary, compare-and-contrast skills, and lesson content.

Past the city, past the suburbs, what do you see?
Farms and woods and smaller towns,
A **rural** community for you and me!
People work in **agriculture** and send the crops along.
Colleges or historic places make the **economy** strong.
A community center or a county fair
are a few things to see.
The rural countryside is a very nice place to be!

© Harcourt

Scaffolding the Content

Preview the Lesson

Have students help you arrange the chairs in rows so the chairs resemble the seats on a bus or train. Then have students take their seats and say: *We are riding on a bus.* Let them bounce up and down as if they are moving. Draw tall buildings on the board, and say: *We are in a city. We go out of the city.* As students watch, erase the tops of the buildings so they become smaller. Say: *We are now in the suburbs. We go out of the suburbs.* As students watch, slowly erase one building, then another, then another, until only a few scattered buildings are left. "Stop" the bus and ask: *Where are we now?* Let students share ideas. Then explain that they have gone to a rural community. Let students draw their journey as you did, showing the change from the city to the suburbs to the country.

- During **Teach**, pp. 57–61
- 25 minutes

Modify Instruction

Hand out the activity sheet (the blackline master page), and help students compare the headings above the circles and the square with the headings in the lesson. Make sure they recognize that the headings are the same. Then explain that students are going to learn about a rural community with a girl named Mallory as their guide.

1. **Searcy, a Rural Community** Help students pronounce the name *Searcy*, using the pronunciation guide on page 56. Then tell students that a rural community is also a small town. Have them listen for things that make a small town special, such as a county fair with games and rides, and a local community center, where people play sports. Ask students to draw and label these things in the first circle on their activity sheets, using the photographs in the lesson for reference.

2. **Urban and Suburban Connections** Remind students how suburban and urban communities are connected, and then explain that rural communities can be connected to these communities in the same ways. Have them trace the arrow leading to the box, then write *Sherwood = suburb* and *Little Rock = city/urban* in the square.

3. **Map on Page 59** Spend some time with students with the map and photographs on page 59. Call out *rural, suburban, urban,* and have students point to the appropriate pictures. Ask students to finger-trace along the map roads to get from place to place.

4. **Other Rural Communities** Tell students that Searcy is not the only kind of rural community. Ask students to explain a university, and say: *Universities and colleges can be in rural communities.* Recall what a historic site is, and say: *Historic sites can be in rural communities.* Invite students to tell about outdoor activities they like to do, and say: *Rural places can be places to enjoy outdoor activities.* Have students write and draw about other rural communities in the bottom circle.

Extend

Remind students that rural communities are connected to suburbs and cities. Help students find the other rural communities mentioned in the lesson on a map. Then ask them to locate the closest urban community and surrounding suburbs. Have students base their map-reading on their experience with the map on page 59.

- After **Teach**, pp. 57–61
- 15 minutes

© Harcourt

Name _____ Date _____

Draw pictures or write about Searcy, a rural community, in the first circle. Draw pictures or write about urban and suburban communities in the square. Draw pictures or write about other rural communities in the second circle.

Rural Communities

Searcy,
a Rural
Community

Urban and Suburban
Communities

Other Rural
Communities

© Harcourt

 School-Home Connection Ask students to take their activity sheets home and to tell their families what they have learned about rural communities. Then have students discuss with their families what kind of community they live in—an urban, suburban, or rural community—and how they know.

Apply and Assess

Write a Diary Entry

Review with students the three kinds of communities they have read about in this chapter. Turn to page 59, and use the pictures there to prompt ideas. Have students point to the community that is most like their own, and explain why they chose that picture. Then tell students that you would like them to write and draw about their community and tell if it is urban, suburban, or rural. Help as necessary. For example:

• During **Close**, p. 61
• 20 minutes

- After drawing their community, beginning students can dictate key words and ideas as you write them on their drawings.

- Intermediate students should be encouraged to write labels and short phrases that tell about the images in their community drawings.

- Advanced students should be encouraged to draw and write complete and interesting sentences that tell about their communities.

Informal Lesson Assessment

	Beginning	Intermediate	Advanced
Task	Student draws a picture of a rural community and dictates labels for it.	Student draws a picture of a rural community, and writes key words and phrases about it.	Student draws a picture of a rural community, and writes complete sentences about it.
Below Expectations	• drawing does not adequately show rural community • student cannot express ideas verbally	• drawing does not show rural community • writing does not reflect drawing • spelling is invented	• drawing does not show rural community • sentences are written incorrectly and do not reflect drawing
Meets Expectations	• drawing shows rural community • student expresses key ideas verbally	• drawing shows rural community • writing reflects drawing • spelling is approximate	• drawing shows rural community • sentence construction is slightly wrong, but sentences reflect drawing
Above Expectations	• drawing shows rural community • student writes some ideas independently	• drawing shows rural community • writing reflects drawing • spelling is correct	• drawing shows rural community • sentences are correct and tell about drawing • sentences are interesting

© Harcourt

Reading Social Studies

Good readers learn to identify text structure and to organize the information that they read. The ability to identify the main idea and the details that support it will help students better understand and remember what they read.

Introduce Main Idea and Details

Explain that the **main idea** is the most important idea in a piece of writing. A **detail** is other information that tells more about the main idea. On the board, write a main idea sentence, such as: *Our laws keep us safe.* Underline the main idea sentence. Next, write some detail sentences: *It is the law to wear a seatbelt in a car. The law also says we must stop at stop signs. We follow these laws to protect ourselves and other people.*

• Before **Main Idea and Details**, p. 76
• 25 minutes

Practice

On the board, write another paragraph with a clear main idea and supporting details. Read your practice paragraph with students, and work with them to identify the main idea. You can help them organize their thoughts by creating a concept web with four surrounding circles. In the center circle, write *The Great Lakes affect the weather.* In the surrounding circles, write *Tiny drops of lake water rise into the air. The winds blow the water to the east. Heavy snow forms. This is lake-effect snow.*

Apply

On the board, create another concept web to record the main idea and details of your practice paragraph. Have students use the concept web to summarize the paragraph, telling about the main idea and the details that support it.

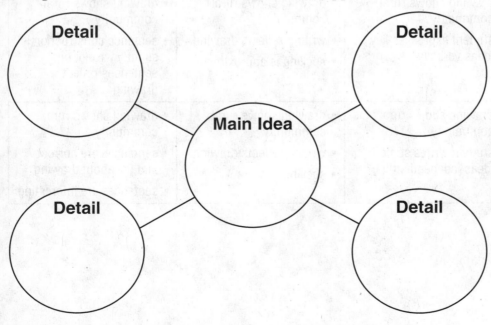

© Harcourt

Build Background

Access Prior Knowledge

Have students say the name of their community. Write it at the bottom of the board. Above it, draw an arrow pointing up. Have students say the name of their state. Write it on the board above the arrow. Above that, draw another arrow, pointing up. Ask students to name the country in which they live. Write *the United States* above the arrow. Explain to students that they are going to learn exactly where their community is.

• Before **Introduce**, p. 82
• 30 minutes

Lesson Vocabulary

Display a map or a globe. Write the word *tool* on the board, and explain that a tool is something that helps us do a job; a **geographic tool** helps us do a job that has to do with geography, or land. Point to the map or the globe, and say: *This is a geographic tool.* Gather students around the globe or map, and label features with sticky notes, such as the **equator,** a **continent,** a **hemisphere,** a **border,** and the **prime meridian.** Encourage students to figure out the meaning and say the name of each as they study the item. Correct and guide as needed. Then point to two places on the globe, and say: *This place is north of that place. This place is south of that place. I have just told you their **relative locations.***

Additional Vocabulary The terms *North Pole* and *South Pole* might mislead students because the word *pole* often refers to a long, cylindrical object. Show students these places on the map or globe, and explain that in geography, a *pole* is the top or bottom of a planet. *The North Pole is at the top of Earth; the South Pole is at the bottom of Earth.* The word *relative* might also be a bit tricky because students will associate a relative with a family member. Explain that here, *relative* is used to describe location. Use context clues to help students understand the meanings of the words and phrases on the right.

aerial	relationship
air	relative
compass rose	taken (from above)
halves	true (shapes)
North Pole/ South Pole	unlike

Cognates As students read the lesson, you may wish to point out cognates such as: **aerial/aéreo, continent/continente, divide/dividir, equator/ ecuador, geographic/geográfico, globe/globo, hemisphere/hemisferio, model/modelo, symbol/símbolo.**

Build Fluency

Read aloud the following rhyme, and point out the words that sound alike. Return to the rhyme throughout the lesson to help develop vocabulary, main idea and details skills, and lesson content.

Where, where, where are you, on a globe or map?
  You can find your community. It's as easy as that!
Continents, hemispheres, and **borders** are places you can be.
  Relative location is where you are compared to me.
Maps, maps, maps and globes are **geographic tools.**
  They can help you find your home.
  They can help you find your school!

© Harcourt

Scaffolding the Content

Preview the Lesson

Students may be unfamiliar with the simple cardinal directions and how to read a compass or a compass rose (the directional indicator on a map). Draw a compass rose on the board, and label it. Say: *A compass rose is a geographic tool.* Then show students a compass rose on a map. Be sure to identify the directions and the symbols that represent the directions. Have students repeat the directions as you point to them on the compass rose.

• During **Teach**, pp. 83–87
• 25 minutes

Ask students why a compass rose might be important. Tell students that a compass rose can help them locate places, like their community. A compass rose also tells them relative location, like *north of, south of,* and so on.

Modify Instruction

Tell students that they are going to learn how geographic tools can help them locate their community. An actual map and globe will be particularly useful for this lesson, so try to have them available. Also, give each student a copy of the activity sheet.

1. **Using Globes** Point to your globe, and have students say: *A globe is a geographic tool.* Have them draw a globe in the "Using Globes" circle of the diagram on the activity sheet. Ask students what a globe shows them, and confirm that a globe shows them the entire Earth. Have them draw and/or write *Earth* in the top box, labeled "Planet." Say: *We all live on Earth.*

2. **Hemispheres** Have students point out the halves of Earth, and explain that these are *hemispheres.* Ask students which two hemispheres their community is in, and agree that it is in the Northern and Western Hemispheres. Have them write *Northern* and *Western* in the "Hemisphere" box of the diagram. Then have students find on the globe the continent for their community. Have them write *North America* in the "Continent" box on the diagram.

3. **Using Maps** Ask students to describe how a map and a globe are different. Have them draw a map in the "Using Maps" circle of the diagram. Say: *A map shows what a place looks like from above.* Ask students if they can see their country on the map. Have them write the *United States* in the "Country" box of the diagram.

4. **Finding Your Location** On a United States map, have students point to lines that show the border between countries and states. Then point out the state in which students live, and have them write the state name in the "State" box. Finally, help students find their community on a map. Say relative locations, such as *north of* or *west of* to guide them. Have them write their community name in the "Community" box.

Extend

Give students another activity sheet. Tell them to choose a community (city or town name) at random on a map or globe. Tell them to fill in the diagram, using the location of the community they chose.

• After **Teach**, pp. 83–87
• 10 minutes

© Harcourt

Name _____ Date _____

DIRECTIONS Fill in the diagram to show the location of your community. Draw a picture of a globe and a map to show these geographic tools.

A Community's Location

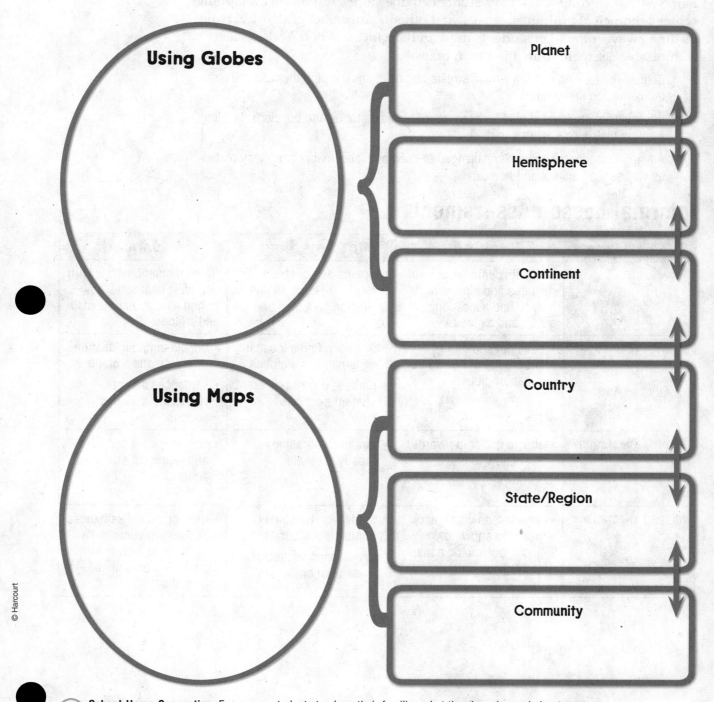

Using Globes

Planet

Hemisphere

Continent

Using Maps

Country

State/Region

Community

School-Home Connection Encourage students to show their families what they have learned about maps, using a map their families have at home and the activity sheet. Tell them to spread out the map and find their community, the borders of their state, and then the country, if possible.

© Harcourt

Apply and Assess

Make a Map

This activity can be challenging for all students, not just English-language learners. To get students thinking, cover a table with drawing paper. Have students stand around the table, and explain that this paper will be a map of their community. Draw in the community's main road, label it, and say its name with the group. Then have students name stores, restaurants, shopping centers, municipal buildings, streets, and other features along this street and leading away from it. Let students draw in their ideas. When students feel comfortable, let them draw their own maps.

• During **Close**, p. 87
• 20 minutes

- Beginning students can draw main streets and buildings, naming them as you write the names on their maps.

- Intermediate students should be encouraged to draw streets and buildings, labeling each on their own or with a partner.

- Advanced students should be challenged to draw and label main community places, as well as their school and homes.

Informal Lesson Assessment

	Beginning	Intermediate	Advanced
Task	Students demonstrate with gestures and single words how to find a location on a map and a globe.	Students demonstrate with phrases how to find a location on a map and a globe.	Students demonstrate with complete sentences how to find a location on a map and a globe.
Below Expectations	• does not show knowledge of how to use a map or globe	• unable to find a location on a map and a globe • phrases do not represent student's actions	• unable to find a location on a map and a globe • sentences do not represent student's actions
Meets Expectations	• able to use some words to tell how to find a location on a map or globe	• student's phrasing is mostly accurate	• sentences are accurate and represent student's actions
Above Expectations	• uses lesson vocabulary words to show how to find a location on a map and a globe	• student's phrasing is completely accurate • uses lesson vocabulary in description	• uses complete sentences and lesson vocabulary to describe how to find a location on a map or globe

© Harcourt

Build Background

Access Prior Knowledge

Ask students to name or draw things, or *features*, in their community that are made by people, like buildings, streets, and parks. Tell them other features are made by nature. Encourage students to name or draw some things in their community made by nature. For example, your community might have a pond, a mountain, a forest, a swamp, or a desert.

• Before **Introduce**, p. 90
• 30 minutes

Lesson Vocabulary

Circle all the words students suggested above, and above the circle, write: **physical features.** Say: *Physical features are made by nature. Physical features are found on Earth.* Have students create a picture dictionary to help them recall physical features. On the board, draw a pointed group of mountains, and label it *mountain range.* Have students copy your image and words in a notebook, saying the words with you. Repeat for **valley, plateau,** and **vegetation.** Point to plants inside or outside, and ask students if there are special times plants grow, or have leaves. Explain that the period when plants grow is called the **growing season.** Have students name plants and animals that live in their area naturally. Explain that all these plants and animals live together in an **ecosystem.** For **erosion,** bring in a salt shaker. Pour some salt onto a tray or plate. Let students gently blow on the salt, noticing the crystals that blow away. Say: *When this process happens to soil, we call it **erosion.** Erosion happens in nature with much bigger things, like mountains. The wind and water can make erosion happen.*

Additional Vocabulary Use context clues to help students understand the meanings of the words on the right.

Cognates As students read the lesson, you may wish to point out cognates such as: **coast/costa, direct/directo, ecosystem/ecosistema, erosion/erosión, island/isla, physical/físico, process/proceso, valley/valle, vegetation/vegetación.**

affected	physical
chain	plains
direct	season
fresh (water)	

Build Fluency

Read aloud the following rhyme, and point out the words that sound alike. Return to the rhyme throughout the lesson to help develop vocabulary, main idea and details skills, and lesson content.

What are some **physical features?**
They are not animals or creatures.
They are plants, water, and land.
Mountain ranges are high, and **valleys** are low.
These are landforms. So are **plateaus.**
Climate and weather are the reason
Vegetation has a special **growing season.**
Rivers, lakes, and oceans are physical features too.
These features make your community special to you!

Scaffolding the Content

Preview the Lesson

A word web will help students organize and retain information about Earth's many physical features. To preview the lesson, pass out copies of the word web blackline master. Create your own word web on the board, too, and write the term *physical features* in the center circle. Look through the chapter with the group, and have students find four headings that relate to physical features. Write each heading in an outer circle and predict what this part of the lesson might be about with students.

• During **Teach**, pp. 91–97
• 30 minutes

Modify Instruction

Tell students that they are going to create a book of physical features, using four more word webs. Pass out the word webs, and begin to explore the lesson.

1. **Land Features** Have students write *Land Features* in the center circle of the first web, below the heading *Physical Features*. Point to various land features in the lesson, and have students identify and describe mountains, valleys, and plateaus. Tell them to write each landform word in an outer circle, and to include an illustration.

2. **Bodies of Water** On another word web, have students write *Bodies of Water* in the center circle. Again, point to various bodies of water in the lesson, and have students identify them, write the names in the outer circles of the web, and illustrate them.

3. **Climate and Weather** On a third word web, have students write *Climate and Weather* in the center circle. Talk about different kinds of weather, and encourage students to write and illustrate these ideas. You might have students draw plants to show different weather and climate, as indicated in the lesson. (For example, cactus for dry, hot weather; palm trees for warm, wet weather.)

4. **Physical Processes** On a fourth word web, have students write *Physical Processes* in the center circle. Pass around the salt again, and have students blow gently as they say *erosion*. Explain that erosion is a physical process. It changes Earth. Have students draw images from the lesson on their word webs that show erosion. In one circle, make sure students write and draw an ecosystem. When finished, staple each student's webs together into a book.

Extend

Give students one more word web. Below the term *Physical Features* in the center circle, have them write *Our Community*. Ask them to recall four different types of physical features from this lesson (land, water, climate and weather, physical processes), and have them write these above each outer circle. Then encourage them to draw or write about the physical features of their community on the web.

• After **Teach**, pp. 91–97
• 10 minutes

© Harcourt

Name _____ Date _____

Fill in this diagram to tell about physical features.

What Are the Physical Features of a Community?

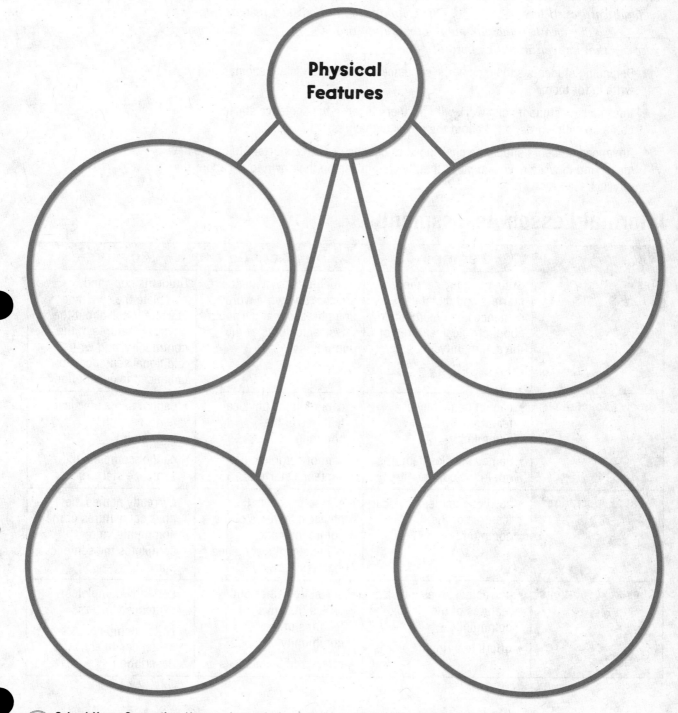

Physical Features

 School-Home Connection Have students take home their word web books of physical features to share with their families. Suggest that students have their families guess the physical features in their community, and then share the last page of their word web books.

Apply and Assess

Write a Description

Students have already organized information about the physical features of their communities on a word web in the "Extend" activity. Let students use their word webs to help organize and write their descriptions. Write sentence starters on the board to prompt their ideas, such as: *Our community has land features. It has _____. Our community has bodies of water. It has _____. The weather and climate in our community is _____. The physical processes that happen in our community are _____.*

• During **Close**, p. 97
• 20 minutes

- Beginning students should copy the sentence starters and dictate endings that you write in for them.
- Intermediate students can work with partners to write the sentence starters and come up with words to tell about the physical features.
- Advanced students should be challenged to use the sentence starters to create new ideas, and to write new sentences that they compose on their own to tell about the physical features.

Informal Lesson Assessment

	Beginning	Intermediate	Advanced
Task	Students copy sentence starters and dictate sentence endings that tell about physical features of the community.	Students copy sentence starters and write words and phrases that tell about physical features of the community.	Students copy and complete the sentence starters to tell about the physical features of the community, and write additional sentences to enhance the description.
Below Expectations	• cannot name physical features of the community • names physical features not in the community	• cannot name physical features of the community • cannot complete the sentence starters	• cannot name physical features of the community • cannot complete the sentence starters
Meets Expectations	• correctly names physical features of the community	• correctly names the physical features of the community and completes the sentence starters	• correctly names the physical features of the community and completes the sentence starters
Above Expectations	• correctly names physical features of the community • offers to write the words	• correctly names and writes the physical features of the community • offers additional ideas	• correctly completes sentence starters • writes complete sentences to enhance description

© Harcourt

Build Background

Access Prior Knowledge

Show students an outline or a map of the United States, and ask them to identify it. Ask them to point out the location of their community. Review the basic cardinal directions by pointing toward areas and having students repeat the directions with you. Point to the Great Lakes and say: *North;* point toward Texas and say: *South;* point toward Virginia and say: *East;* and point toward California and say: *West.* Then ask students to choose the direction that best describes their community's location within the United States. Say: *Is our community north, south, east, or west?*

• Before **Introduce**, p. 102
• 20 minutes

Lesson Vocabulary

Show students items you have in class for art projects. You might also show students coins you save. Pick up a trash can, and say: *I do not put this in the trash. I save it.* Pantomime *not* putting something in the trash. Do this with several items, asking students to repeat your words. Say: *I do not put this in the trash. What do I do with it?* When students become familiar with the word *save,* write it on the board, then write *save = **preserve**.* Repeat the sentences from above, and this time have students say the word *preserve* instead of *save.* Then go on to have students create original sentences with *preserve.*

Additional Vocabulary The word *storytelling* might be confusing to some students. Write it on the board, and circle the word *story.* Show students fiction books, and say: *These are stories. I tell you a story.* Underline the word *telling.* Have students say what *storytelling* might mean, and confirm that *storytelling* is telling stories. Tell them to look for this and other vocabulary words as they read. Review other words in the margin in the context of the lesson, and have students make their own sentences.

depends on	geographically
develop	relative
feature	storytelling
geographer	tied to

Cognates As students read the lesson, you may wish to point out cognates such as: **climate/clima, culture/cultura, depend on/depender de, divide/dividir, economics/economía, geographer/geógrafo, music/música, region/región, relative/relativo.**

Build Fluency

Read aloud the following rhyme, and point out the words that sound alike. Return to the chant throughout the lesson to help develop vocabulary, main idea and details skills, and lesson content. As students call out each region, have them indicate location with hand motions.

Divide it! Separate it! Make five large parts!
Our country has regions. Where should we start?
Southwest! Middle West! Don't forget the West!
Three big regions. What is left?
Northeast! Southeast! That makes five!
Five separate regions! One big country to divide!
Southwest! Middle West! Don't forget the West!
Northeast! Southeast! Five regions are best!

© Harcourt

Scaffolding the Content

Preview the Lesson

• During **Teach**, pp. 103–105
• 20 minutes

In "Access Prior Knowledge," you reviewed with students the cardinal directions *north, south, east,* and *west.* Now, introduce students to the directions of *northeast, southeast, southwest,* and *northwest.* Draw a large compass rose on the board. Point to north, but do not identify it, and have students name it. Confirm by writing the word on your compass rose. Continue in this way with south, east, and west.

On the compass rose, point to the spot between north and east, and ask students what you might call this direction. Elicit ideas, and confirm that it is northeast. Write this direction name on the compass rose. Continue in the same way with southeast, southwest, and northwest.

Modify Instruction

Give each student a copy of the United States outline map from the blackline master page. Point out the lighter lines, and ask students what these lines show. Agree that they show the borders between states. Let students point to their state. Then point to the heavier, darker lines, and ask students what these lines show. Explain that these lines show the five large regions of the United States. Begin to explore the chapter.

1. **The Regions** Say the regions *Northeast, Southeast, West,* and *Southwest.* Tell students to rely on what they know about these directions, and challenge them to locate each region on their maps. Have them label each region. Point out that one region has not been named, and have them find the name of that region on page 103. Tell them to write *Midwest* in the last region on their maps. Ask students why the names of these regions are good names. Agree that the names tell the location of each region.

2. **Other Regions** Ask students if the United States could have other ways to divide or separate parts of the country into regions. After students offer ideas, show students a topographical map of the United States, and point out some landforms, such as the Rocky Mountains, the Everglades, and the Sonoran Desert. Have students point out other landforms they see. Then point to the Appalachian Mountains. Explain that these mountains form a region called Appalachia. Ask them to identify the geographic region of Kentucky (the Southeast). Invite students to draw in the Appalachian mountains on their maps, and have them repeat: *The Appalachian mountains make a region.*

Extend

• After **Teach**, pp. 103–105
• 10 minutes

Have students identify the geographic region of their state, and then help them consider any other region their state or community might be a part of. Using the topographical map, have students point to any nearby landforms and draw those landforms on their maps. Also have students describe the climate where they live. Then lead students to discover another regional name for the area they live in.

DIRECTIONS Write the name of the region in each space on the map.

Our Country's Regions

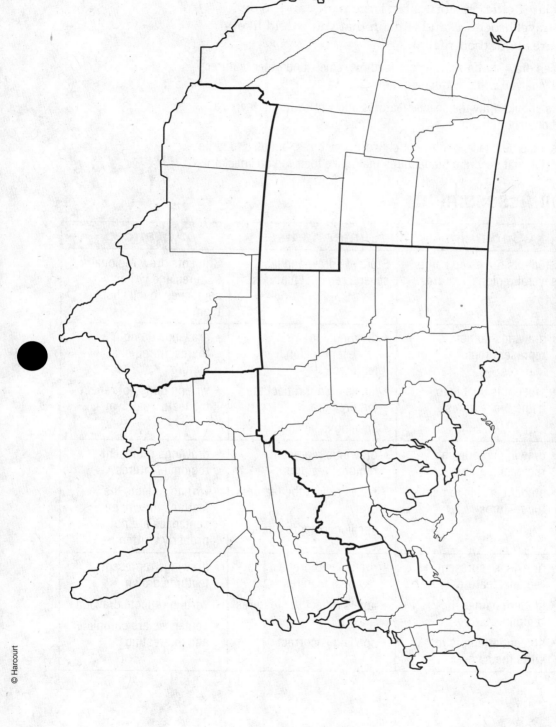

© Harcourt

 School-Home Connection Have students take their maps home to share with their families. Tell them to show their families the location of their state and community, and to say the name of the region. Then with their families, have students name other places that are in their region.

Apply and Assess

Write a Travel Brochure

Begin a word web, and invite students to name features that make their region special, such as large cities, historic sites, large parks, and so on. Then show students a travel brochure, and explain that you would like them to create a brochure about their region.

• During **Close**, p. 105
• 30 minutes

- Beginning students can draw landforms, climate features, cities, and other features, identifying them orally as you write them down.

- Intermediate students should draw the special features and work with partners to write labels and captions about them.

- Advanced students should be challenged to not only draw pictures, but also to write sentences or paragraphs that describe the features that make their region special.

Informal Lesson Assessment

	Beginning	Intermediate	Advanced
Task	Students draw and name several regional features.	Students draw and label several regional features.	Students draw regional features and write sentences to tell about them.
Below Expectations	• drawings do not represent regional features • student is unable to name the features	• drawings do not represent regional features • labels do not reflect the features drawn • spelling is invented	• drawings do not represent regional features • writing does not reflect the features drawn
Meets Expectations	• drawings represent regional features • student is able to name the features	• drawings represent regional features • labels reflect the features drawn • spelling is approximate	• drawings represent regional features • writing reflects the features drawn, but sentences are not properly written
Above Expectations	• drawings represent regional features • student names the regional features • student attempts to write the names	• drawings represent regional features • labels reflect the features drawn • spelling is correct	• drawings represent features drawn • writing reflects drawings • sentences are complete and interesting

Build Background

Access Prior Knowledge

Write the word *nature* on the board, and have students explain it in their own words. Ask them to draw pictures that show parts of nature, such as trees, flowers, grass, birds, insects, water, clouds, rocks, and so on. Have students share their drawings, challenging them to name what they have drawn. Use students' drawings to form a word web on the board, with the word *nature* in the center and students' drawings placed around it. Praise students on their ability to know what is found in nature.

• Before **Introduce**, p. 106
• 30 minutes

Lesson Vocabulary

Write the word *nature* on the board, and encourage students to recognize it. As students watch, change the word to *natural resources.* Explain that *natural* means "having to do with nature." *Resources* are things we use; **natural resources** are things we use that come from nature. Review the student pictures, and discuss items people might use. For each item, write and say: *This is a natural resource.* Call attention to a picture of a rock. Say: *This is a rock. A rock is a* **mineral.** *A mineral is a natural resource.* Point out a picture of trees or wood. Ask students what would happen if wood were on fire. Agree that it would be hot, or give off heat. Say: *Heat is energy. A natural resource that makes energy is called* **fuel.** *Wood is a fuel.* Cover the wood, and say: *We have no more wood. How can we make more?* Say: *To make more is to* renew. *Wood is a* **renewable** *resource. We can make more of it by planting new trees.* Then help students understand that some resources, like coal, are **nonrenewable.** That is, we cannot make more of it.

Additional Vocabulary Review the words in the margin in the context of the lesson, and assist students to make their own sentences.

Cognates As students read the lesson, you may wish to point out cognates such as: **energy/energía, example/ejemplo, mineral/mineral, natural/natural, naturalist/naturalista, nature/naturaleza, rich/rica,-o.**

choicest	replaced
laid	rich
living resources	steady

Build Fluency

Read aloud this chant. Return to it throughout the lesson to help develop vocabulary, main idea and details skills, and lesson content.

Natural resources are things we use. Can you name them?
Trees and land and water, too, are natural resources that we use!
Some of these will grow again, grow again, grow again.
Some of these will grow again. They are **renewable!**
We use **minerals** only once, only once, only once.
We use minerals only once. **They're nonrenewable.**

© Harcourt

Scaffolding the Content

Preview the Lesson

Point to objects around the room, and have students say what natural resource the objects were made from, or which natural resource they see. For example:

- During **Teach**, pp. 107–109
- 30 minutes

- Desks, chairs, paper, pencils, boxes: Trees/wood.
- Classroom plants, leaves, flowers: Plants.
- Water at a sink, water fountain, aquarium: Water.
- Rocks, copper coins, salt, jewelry: Minerals.

Start a collection of such objects, point to them, and have students repeat: *Natural resources. These things are made from natural resources.* Ask students how else we might use natural resources, and list their ideas on the board.

Modify Instruction

Tell students that they are going to learn about different natural resources. Have students review what the term *natural resources* means. Then hand out the activity sheet from the next page for students to complete as they explore the lesson.

1. **Our Resources** Have students find the word *trees* in the first paragraph of this section. Say: *Trees are a natural resource.* Have students draw and label a tree in the center square of the diagram on the activity sheet. Have them point to objects in the room that we get from trees. Have students look for the word *land* in the second paragraph. Ask students how we use land, and then have them draw and label *land* in the center box of the diagram. Continue in this way with water and minerals, having students add them to the chart.

2. **Types of Resources: Renewable and Nonrenewable** Explain that these resources can be grouped in different ways. Ask students to explain the difference between renewable and nonrenewable. Have them recite the chant to recall which natural resources are renewable, and have them find these resources in the first paragraph of this section. Tell them to draw plants and animals in the corresponding box of the chart. Have them do the same for nonrenewable.

3. **Types of Resources: Living and Nonliving** Point to yourself, and say: *Living.* Point to a desk, and say: *Nonliving.* Do the same with a piece of chalk, and a book. Ask students to explain the difference between living and nonliving. Then say: *Natural resources can be living or nonliving.* Point to items students drew in the center box of their diagrams, and have them identify each as living or nonliving. Tell students to draw each in the proper box of their diagrams.

Extend

Have students copy these sentences: *I use natural resources. I use _____.* Tell students to complete the last sentence with a natural resource they use. Then have students draw a picture of themselves using that natural resource. Let students combine their pages into a "Natural Resources" book.

- After **Teach**, pp. 107–109
- 20 minutes

Name _____ Date _____

DIRECTIONS In the big center box, write or draw natural resources. Then sort the natural resources into the smaller boxes.

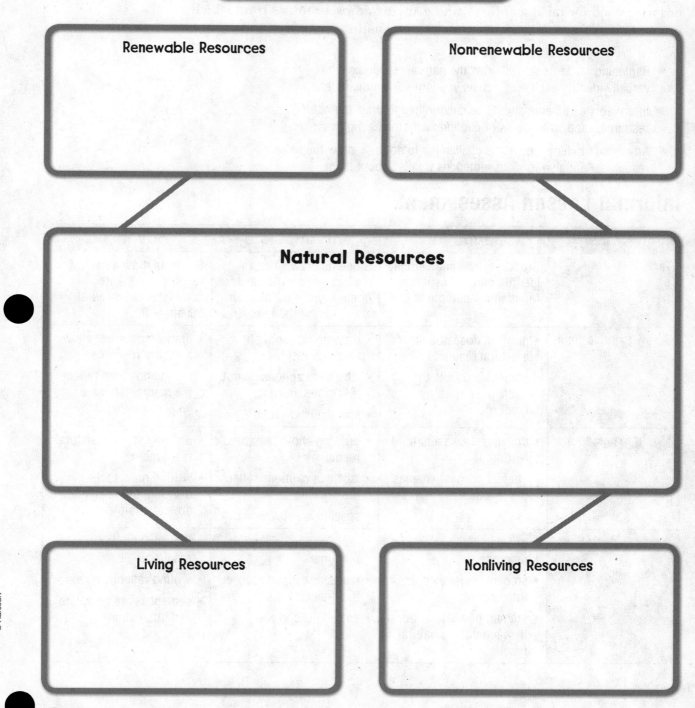

What Are Natural Resources?

Renewable Resources

Nonrenewable Resources

Natural Resources

Living Resources

Nonliving Resources

School-Home Connection Ask students to take their diagrams home to share with their families. Ask students to discuss with their families which natural resources they use. Have students draw pictures to show which natural resources they use and how they use them.

Apply and Assess

Draw a Picture

• During **Close**, p. 109
• 30 minutes

Point out to students that they have named natural resources that they use. Now have them think about natural resources that are found in their community. Guide their ideas by naming ponds or reservoirs where the community might get their water, for example, or forests used for lumber, or farms used for raising animals and growing crops, or mines from which minerals are dug. Ask students to draw these natural resources and write about them.

- Beginning students should draw the natural resources, and verbally identify each resource as you write down their ideas.

- Intermediate students should be encouraged to draw the natural resources, and write labels or captions with the help of partners.

- Advanced students should be challenged to not only draw the natural resources, but also to write sentences that tell about them.

Informal Lesson Assessment

	Beginning	Intermediate	Advanced
Task	Students draw and verbally identify natural resources found in the community.	Students draw a natural resource and write labels or captions to tell about it.	Students draw a natural resource and write complete sentences to tell about it.
Below Expectations	• drawing does not show a natural resource • student is unable to name the natural resource	• drawing does not show a natural resource • labels or captions do not reflect the drawing • spelling is invented	• drawing does not show a natural resource • writing does not reflect the natural resource
Meets Expectations	• drawing shows a natural resource • student correctly names the resource	• drawing shows a natural resource • labels or captions reflect the drawing • spelling is approximate	• drawing shows a natural resource • writing reflects the drawing, but sentences are not complete
Above Expectations	• drawing shows a natural resource • student correctly names the resource • student offers to write the name of the natural resource	• drawing shows a natural resource • labels or captions reflect the drawing • spelling is correct	• drawing shows a natural resource • writing reflects drawing • sentences are complete and interesting

© Harcourt

Build Background

Access Prior Knowledge

Have students recall words they connect with nature. Say key words, such as *weather, climate, landforms,* and have students explain what they mean. Write these words on the board under the heading *physical features*. Say: *Physical features are made by nature. What other physical features do you know?* Below the heading, list additional ideas students suggest.

• Before **Introduce**, p. 114
• 20 minutes

Lesson Vocabulary

Add a second column to the chart, with the heading **human features.** Say: *Human features are made by people. What human features do you know?* To prompt ideas, you might show pictures of buildings, bridges, and roads. Above your chart, write the word **environment.** Say the word for the group several times, asking students to say it with you. Explain that physical features and human features make up an environment. Pantomime being cold, and say: *Some environments are cold.* Put on a sweater or coat, and say: *People **adapt** to their environment. They change to make their environment more comfortable. Putting on a coat or sweater is one way of adapting.* Then turn the lights on and off, and ask students what makes the lights work. Students will probably say *electricity.* Explain: *Electricity comes from **energy.** Heat has energy.* Write *energy* on the board, and have students think of ways we get heat (from the sun, from burning wood, oil, and so on). Finally, say: *The wind is too strong. It rains too much. It snows too much. These things can cause **natural disasters.*** Write the term on the board, and help students recognize the word *nature.*

Additional Vocabulary Review words or phrases in the margin in the context of the lesson, and have students make their own sentences as they are able.

Cognates As students read the lesson, you may wish to point out cognates such as: **adapt/adaptar, affect/afectar, disaster/desastre, electricity/electricidad.**

affect	landscape
damage	loose
herd	store
knock down	ways of

Build Fluency

Read aloud the following rhyme, and point out the words that sound alike. Return to the chant throughout the lesson to help develop vocabulary, main idea and details skills, and lesson content.

People **adapt** to where they live, the climate and the land,
Some wear special clothes or have lawns made out of sand.
When it's cold we burn coal and gas or use heat from the sun.
Energy is how we get the power to make things run.
When it's hot we dream of falling snow.
When **natural disasters** strike, we must have a safe place to go.

© Harcourt

Scaffolding the Content

Preview the Lesson

• During **Teach**, pp. 115–118
• 25 minutes

In order for students to fully grasp the lesson, they need to recall the meaning of the word *affect*. Write *affect* on the board, and say it with the group. Explain that *affect* is similar to *cause*. Then demonstrate how something can affect another thing. For example, place some tall objects on a table, and then shake the table. Ask students to tell what happened. Then write the word *environment* with the word *affect*. Point to each word, and say: *The environment affects people. It affects communities, too.* Draw an arrow pointing from *environment* to *affect*. This previews what students will see on the graphic organizer.

Modify Instruction

Pass out the blackline master, and have students recognize the words *environment* and *affects*. Then work with students to fill out the diagram.

1 **Our Environment** First, review with students that the environment is made of physical features and human features. Then have students finger-trace a path from the box with the words *The environment* along the arrow with the word *affects,* to the box labeled *where people live.* In this box, ask students to draw pictures of places where people might live, such as on mountains, at the beach, in the city, or in deserts. Ask students how people might need to adapt if they lived in these environments. If necessary, suggest categories such as homes, transportation, food, and so on.

2 **Adapting to the Environment** Have students finger-trace a path along the second arrow to the second box. Have them read the title, and have them repeat: *The environment affects how people live. People choose their houses, clothing, and transportation to adapt to the environment.* In this box, have students draw and label clothing for different environments, houses for different environments, and transportation for different environments.

3 **People and Disasters** Have students finger-trace a path along the third arrow to the last box. Have them read the title, and have them repeat: *The environment affects people. Quick changes in the environment are called natural disasters.* Natural disasters affect people. Have students draw pictures of natural disasters in the third box. Have students label each picture. Then ask how people could adapt to these natural disasters.

Extend

• After **Teach**, pp. 115–118
• 20 minutes

Let students create mobiles that show their environment and ways people adapt to it. Give each student a paper plate, and ask them to draw a picture that shows the environment in which they live. For example, if the community is in the desert, they could draw a cactus or sand dune. Then have students draw and cut out objects that show how people adapt, such as types of clothing, types of homes, and types of transportation. If possible, have them attach the cutouts to the edge of the paper plate with string or yarn.

© Harcourt

Name _____ Date _____

DIRECTIONS Draw pictures to show how the environment affects people.

People and the Environment

... where people live

The environment . . .

affects →

... how people live

affects →

affects →

... people and natural disasters

School-Home Connection Have students take this page home, and explain what environment means and how the environment affects people. Students can also share their mobiles with their families.

Apply and Assess

Write a Story

• During **Close**, p. 118
• 30 minutes

Brainstorm with students environments that are different from their own. Encourage students to explain the differences. Then tell each student to choose an environment to write about. Guide students as necessary.

- Beginning students can draw the chosen environment, as well as a family who lives there. Have the student point to and verbally express the adaptations the family must make.

- Intermediate students can draw pictures to prompt ideas. Encourage them also to write short sentences that tell about the environment and how a family adapts to it.

- Advanced students should be challenged to write their story in complete and interesting sentences, focusing on a main character and the environment.

Informal Lesson Assessment

	Beginning	Intermediate	Advanced
Task	Student draws an environment with people and explains how the environment affects people.	Student draws an environment with people and writes short sentences about how the environment affects people.	Student writes a story that tells how a new environment affects a family.
Below Expectations	• drawing does not show environment and people • student is unable to express ideas verbally	• drawing does not show environment or people • sentences do not tell about drawing	• story does not tell about environment • story does not tell about effects • sentence construction is poor
Meets Expectations	• drawing shows environment and people • student expresses ideas verbally • ideas are slightly incorrect	• drawing shows environment and people • sentences tell about drawing • sentences tell how environment affects the people.	• story tells about the environment's effects on family • sentence construction is adequate
Above Expectations	• drawing shows environment and people • student expresses ideas verbally • ideas are correct	• drawing shows environment and people • sentences tell about drawing • sentences tell how the environment affects the people	• story tells about environment's effects on family • sentences are complete and interesting

© Harcourt

Build Background

Access Prior Knowledge

Show students pictures of human features, such as houses, roads, stores, bridges, lampposts, and mailboxes. Point to each feature, and have students recall the word. Ask students what all these things have in common. Agree that people make all these things. Discuss why people create human features.

• Before **Introduce**, p. 122
• 30 minutes

Lesson Vocabulary

Point to all the objects students just named, and explain that when people add things to the land, they change it. Say: *They **modify** the environment.* Write *modify* on the board and say it with the group. Say: *Modify means to change.* Point to the pictures of the Panama Canal on pages 122 and 123, and say: *canal.* Write the word on a self-stick note, and put it on the picture. Have students do the same. Follow the same procedure for **terrace** on page 124, **irrigation** on page 124, and **dam** on page 126. Indicate the water on page 126, and write the word *reservoir* on the board. Say: *A reservoir is a place to save water. A reservoir has water that we drink.* Ask them if they think this lake is a reservoir and explain why or why not. Finally, draw a simple group of mountains on the board, then draw an arch at the base of a mountain to represent a tunnel. Say: *People make **tunnels**. Tunnels go underground or through mountains. Tunnels modify the environment.* Point to other words students have learned, and have them replace each word in the same sentence: *People make _____. _____ modify the environment.*

Additional Vocabulary Review words or phrases in the margin in the context of the lesson.

Cognates As students read the lesson, you may wish to point out cognates such as: **canal/canal, cement/cemento, control/controlar, gravel/grava, irrigation/irrigación, machine/máquina, mine/mina, modify/modificar, project/proyecto, structure/estructura, terrace/terraza, tunnel/túnel, turbine/turbina.**

clear (verb)
look (noun)
meet their needs
mine (noun)
pit
speed up
supplies

Build Fluency

Read aloud the following rhyme, and point out the words that sound alike. Return to the rhyme throughout the lesson to help develop vocabulary, main idea and details skills, and lesson content.

People build **terraces** so planting never stops.
They set up **irrigation** to water their crops.
A **dam** controls water and how it flows.
A **reservoir** has drinking water. This is good to know!
People **modify** the environment—yes they do!
People **modify** the environment—can you?

© Harcourt

Scaffolding the Content

Preview the Lesson

Help students understand the meaning of each heading in this lesson.

• During **Teach**, pp. 122–127
• 30 minutes

- **Transportation** Ask students to say in their own words what transportation means. On a sheet of paper, have students write the word *transportation.* Then ask them to draw images that show ways people get from place to place.

Continue in this way with *farming, mining, water,* and *electricity.* Tell students that they will learn more about each as they explore the lesson.

Modify Instruction

Give each student a copy of the graphic organizer. Have them read the title, and then have them recognize the headings on the diagram as the same headings they wrote on their pictures in "Preview the Lesson." Then begin reviewing the lesson.

1 **Transportation** Ask students to look through the lesson for pictures of a new type of transportation that they did not mention before—the canal on pages 122–123. Encourage students to draw and label a canal on their diagrams, and to explain in their own words what the picture shows and how a canal helps with transportation. Then invite students to help you crumple up large sheets of paper to form a mountain. Ask students how they could move through the mountain. If possible, place a paper towel tube through the paper mountain, and identify it as a tunnel. Have students draw and label a tunnel on their diagrams.

2 **Farming and Mining** Viewing the photographs on page 124, have students describe terrace farming and irrigation in their own words. Ask them to draw and label terrace farming and irrigation on their diagrams. Then ask students to tell another reason why people might dig. Have them describe the mine they see on page 125. Show students a stone, and have them make the connection that stones and other minerals come from mines. Have students draw a mine and minerals on their diagrams.

3 **Water and Electricity** Viewing the photograph on page 126, have students explain how a dam affects water. Encourage them to draw a dam and a reservoir on their diagrams. Then ask students to describe the power of fast-moving water or a strong wind. Say: *Fast-moving water and strong wind can make electricity.* Have students draw water and a dam and wind and a wind turbine on their diagrams.

Extend

Cover a table with tan or brown mural paper. Run a strip of blue paper along the length, in the middle. Point to the brown paper and say: *This is the land.* Point to the blue paper and say: *This is the water.* Then let students draw pictures or create models to show how people modify the land. Have them label each change.

• After **Teach**, pp. 122–127
• 30 minutes

Name _____ Date _____

DIRECTIONS Draw and label pictures to show how people modify the environment.

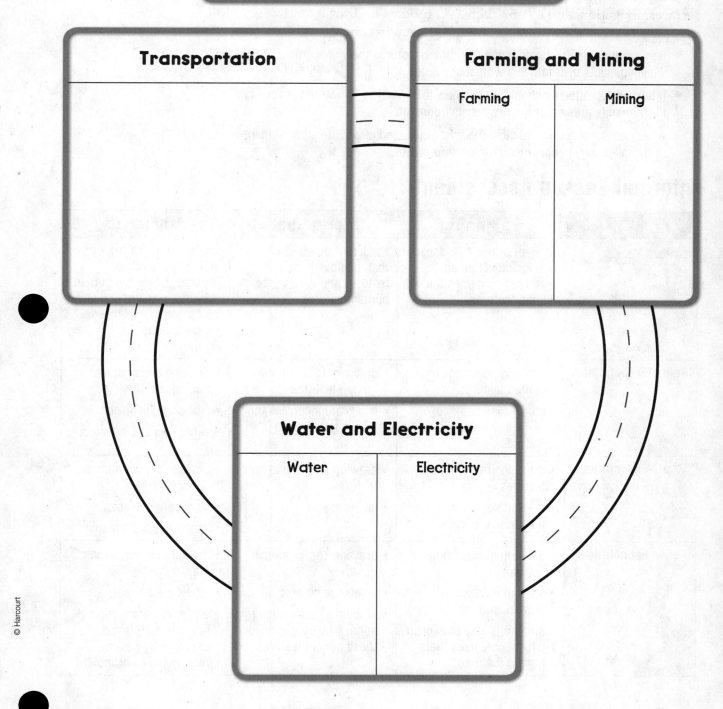

How People Modify the Environment

Transportation

Farming and Mining

Farming	Mining

Water and Electricity

Water	Electricity

 School-Home Connection Before students show their diagrams to their families, have them ask their families to name ways that people change the environment. Then have students share their diagrams, checking to see which items on their diagrams their families named.

© Harcourt

Apply and Assess

Draw a Picture

Start a word web on the board, with *How We Modify the Environment* in the center circle. Ask students to name human features that modify the environment, and write their ideas in the outer circles of the web. Allow all reasonable answers, such as roads, bridges, houses, canals, tunnels, terraces, irrigation, and so on. Then ask students to draw a landscape, and to add pictures that show how we modify the environment.

• During **Close**, p. 127
• 20 minutes

- Beginning students should name the human features they have drawn while you label their drawing with sticky notes.

- Intermediate students should write labels to show they know the vocabulary for human features that modify the environment.

- Advanced students should label their drawings, and also write a few sentences that explain why people modify the environment.

Informal Lesson Assessment

	Beginning	Intermediate	Advanced
Task	Student draws a landscape that includes human features and names the human features.	Student draws a landscape that includes human features and labels the human features.	Student draws a landscape that includes human features, labels the human features, and writes a few sentences to explain why people modify the environment.
Below Expectations	• drawing does not show human features • student is unable to name any human features	• drawing does not show human features • labels are incorrect and do not reflect the drawing	• drawing does not show human features • labels are incorrect • sentences are incorrect
Meets Expectations	• drawing shows human features • student names the human features	• drawing shows human features • labels are correct	• drawing shows human features • labels are correct • sentences are adequate
Above Expectations	• drawing shows human features • student names the human features • student is able to explain why people need these human features	• drawing shows human features • labels are correct • student offers ideas about why people need these human features	• drawing shows human features • labels are correct • sentences are complete and interesting and explain why people modify the environment

© Harcourt

Build Background

Access Prior Knowledge

On a large sheet of poster or chart paper, draw a very simple landscape. Invite students to draw something that people add to the land, such as a house, a farm, a bridge, or a road. Have students say the names of the objects they draw, and explain why people add them to the land.

* Before **Introduce**, p. 128
* 20 minutes

Lesson Vocabulary

Display the following sentences. Have pairs of students work together to say or write a definition for each vocabulary word based on context clues. Discuss the words that provide context clues. Students can look up the words in the Glossary to verify their meanings.

1 People can change a place, or the environment. **Pollution** is bad for the environment. Garbage and smoke from cars and chimneys cause pollution. This makes our air, land, and water dirty.

2 When we are finished with something, we throw it away. It becomes trash. Some trash can be recycled. For example, we can **recycle** writing paper to make paper bags.

3 Paper comes from trees. When we recycle paper, we save trees. When we practice **conservation**, we help the environment.

Additional Vocabulary Review the words or phrases in the margin in the context of the lesson, and have students make their own sentences.

Cognates As students read the lesson, you may wish to point out cognates such as: **aluminum/aluminio, conservation/conservación, electric/eléctric-o/-a, gasoline/gasolina, hybrid/híbrid-o/-a, motor/motor, pollution/polución, problem/problema, protect/proteger, recycle/reciclar.**

care
landfill
last longer
set aside
waste

Build Fluency

Read aloud the following rhyme, and point out the words that sound alike. Return to the chant to help develop vocabulary, main idea and details skills, and lesson content. This rhyme can be loosely sung to "I've Been Working on the Railroad."

We should practice **conservation**—every single day.
We should practice conservation. It's the cleanest, safest way.
Pollution makes air bad and dirty, the sky and water, too.
People make all this pollution. We must try something new.
What can we do? What can we do?
What can we do for the environment?
What can we do? What can we do?
We can **recycle** to show that we care!

© Harcourt

Scaffolding the Content

Preview the Lesson

Have students view the pictures in the lesson, and challenge them to apply the vocabulary words to each picture. For example:

| • During **Teach**, pp. 128–131
| • 20 minutes

pp. 128–129 Have students describe as best they can the pictures on these pages. Say: *Which word best tells about these pictures*—pollution, conservation, or recycle? Agree that pollution best describes the pictures, and have students explain why.

p. 130 Have students describe what they see in these pictures. Ask: *Which words best tell about these pictures*—pollution, conservation, *or* recycle? Agree that *conservation* and *recycle* best tell about these pictures.

Modify Instruction

Tell students that they will learn more about the words pollution, conservation, and recycle. Pass out the blackline master. Read the main heading on the chart, and explain that it is the same as the title of the lesson: *Caring for Our Environment*. Then have students find the first heading in the lesson on the chart and begin.

1. **Controlling Pollution** Ask students what "causes of pollution" might mean, and agree that it means things that make pollution. Have students find the word *trash* in the text, and draw pictures of trash in the "causes" box of their charts. Have them look for the word *factories.* Have students explain what factories do, and agree that factories make things; some factories make electricity. Ask students to draw factories on their charts. Also draw a car, showing its exhaust. Have students identify what makes pollution in that picture, and ask them to draw similar pictures on their charts. Then ask students how we can make less pollution. In the "Reducing Pollution" part of their charts, have them draw cars that make no exhaust, and have them write *hybrid cars* on their charts.

2. **Conserving Our Resources** Have students locate this heading on their charts and then the heading "Reusing Resources." Ask students which word they learned that means *reusing,* and have them find *recycle* in the text. Tell them to draw recycling bins and objects to be recycled in this part of the chart. They can also draw themselves reusing an object, like a shopping bag or scrap paper. Use the last part of the chart for "Extend."

3. **A Plan for the Future** Ask students what a *plan* is. Agree that a plan is something you will do later; it is usually well organized and has steps. Have students talk with each other, and think about a plan they could follow to care for the environment. Invite students to work together to write and draw their ideas in this last box of the chart.

Extend

Invite groups of students to come up with a plan to help the environment. They can start by listing classroom or household items to recycle and then move on to things they and their families can do at home to reduce pollution. Invite each group to create a poster that outlines their plan, and present it to the class.

| • After **Teach**, pp. 128–131
| • 15 minutes

© Harcourt

Name _____ Date _____

DIRECTIONS Complete the chart to show how people hurt the environment. Complete the chart to show how people help the environment, too.

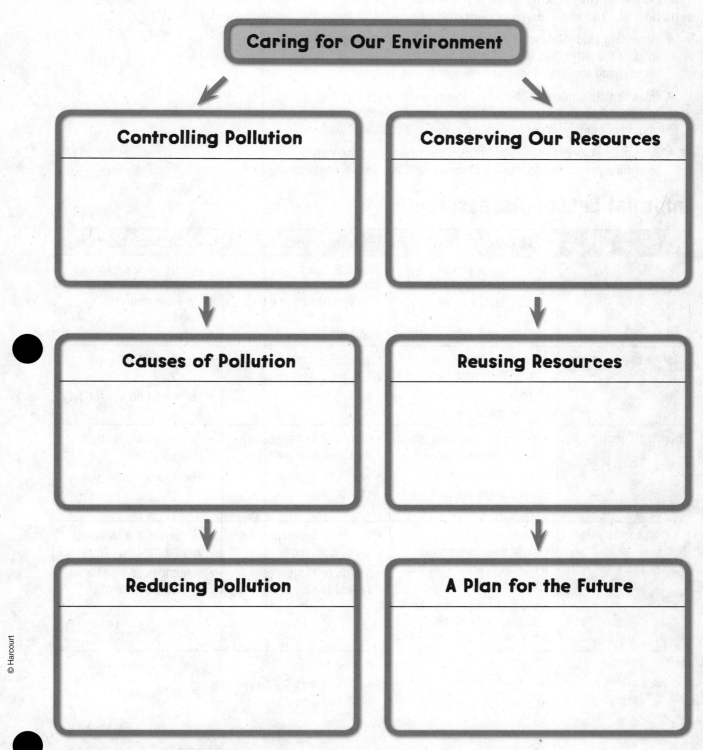

Caring for Our Environment

Controlling Pollution

Conserving Our Resources

Causes of Pollution

Reusing Resources

Reducing Pollution

A Plan for the Future

School-Home Connection Encourage students to share their flow charts with their families. Have them first explain how people hurt the environment and then how people care for the environment. Let students add ideas to their charts that their families have about how to care for the environment.

© Harcourt

Apply and Assess

Write a Persuasive Letter

On the board, set up a letter format that includes the date, the greeting, the body, and the closing. Then tell students they will write a letter that tells how we hurt the environment and how we can help the environment.

• During **Close**, p. 131
• 20 minutes

- Beginning students should dictate ideas to you. Encourage them to start the letter, and then fill in the body of the letter with students' ideas. Read the letter together.

- Intermediate students should be encouraged to work together to write ideas about hurting and caring for the environment. They should compose simple sentences, such as: *Pollution is bad.*

- Advanced students should be encouraged to work independently to write a persuasive letter with complete and interesting sentences.

Informal Lesson Assessment

	Beginning	Intermediate	Advanced
Task	Students use pictures and words on a cause-and-effect chart to show how people care for the environment.	Students use words and phrases on a cause-and-effect chart to show how people care for the environment.	Students write sentences to describe three ways people can help the environment.
Below Expectations	• words and pictures do not reflect task • student does not understand the task	• words are incorrect • words do not reflect topic	• sentences are simple or incorrect • sentences do not reflect topic
Meets Expectations	• words and pictures tell about the environment • student uses chart to show ways we care for the environment	• words or sentences are written correctly • words or sentences reflect topic	• sentences are written correctly • sentences reflect topic
Above Expectations	• student adequately expresses ideas about how people care for the environment • student offers to write some words on his or her own	• words or sentences are written correctly • words or sentences reflect topic	• sentences are complete and interesting • sentences convey variety of ideas in lesson

Developing Academic Language

Sequence is the order in which things happen. When students read social studies texts, it is important for them to note sequence. The ability to recognize the words that signal sequence will help students keep track of and remember important events.

Introduce Sequence

Show students one week on a calendar. You might enlarge the week or draw a calendar week on poster paper. Point to each day, and encourage students to echo the name for that day. Then cut the days apart, mix them up, and place them on a tabletop in the wrong sequence. Ask students whether the days are in the right order.

- Before **Sequence**, p. 148
- 25 minutes

Confirm that the days of the week are out of order, or out of **sequence.** Write *order = sequence* on the board. Say: *Sequence is the order that things happen. When authors want to show sequence, they use the words* first, second, *and* third. *They can also use* next, then, *and* after. Using the calendar, encourage students to use signal words to talk about the order of the days of the week. Model how to use language, such as the following:

> **First comes Sunday, then comes Monday.**
> **Tuesday is after Monday.**
> **The last day of the week is Saturday.**

Practice

Together, write a paragraph on the board that summarizes major events of a typical school morning. Include such tasks as arriving at school, hanging up coats/backpacks, taking attendance, and so on. On the board, write a list that summarizes the morning's tasks. Model using the words *first, second, third, next, then,* and *finally,* as appropriate.

Apply

Display the time line below on the board, and have students copy it onto a piece of paper. Give students simple nonfiction books, magazine articles, or news stories that show a clear sequence of events. Begin by helping students find the sequential events, use signal words to describe them, and record them on the time line. Gradually provide less help until students can do it alone.

© Harcourt

| First | Second | Next | Last |

Build Background

Access Prior Knowledge

Show or draw a picture of yourself at a younger age. Have students identify things about you that have changed, such as height, and things that have stayed the same, such as eye color. Point out that people change. Tell students that communities change, too. Show pictures of your community from the past. Ask students to point out things that are different in the present.

• Before **Introduce**, p. 156
• 25 minutes

Lesson Vocabulary

Write the word **decade** on the board. Explain that a decade is ten years. Ask students to predict what they will be like in a decade. Encourage them to use the word by asking questions. For example: *In a decade, will you be out of high school?* Then write **century** on the board. Explain that a century is one hundred years. Ask questions using the word. For example: *Do most people live a century? Can it take a century for a tree to get very tall?* Finally, write **continuity** on the board. Explain that it comes from the word continue, which means "to go on." Return to the community pictures from "Access Prior Knowledge." Have students find examples of things that have stayed the same over the years.

Additional Vocabulary Introduce the multiple-meaning words in the margin. For example, students may know that *mine* talks about "something that belongs to me." Explain that a *mine* is also a place where people dig up valuable stones and metals. In addition, explain the meaning of the phrases related to time. Use sentences such as: *You will get taller* as time passes. Continue to introduce the words and phrases at the right in the same way.

affect	present
as time passes	put out (fire)
events	rebuilt
mine	take place
over time	time to come

Cognates As students read the lesson, you may wish to point out cognates such as: **decade/década, continuity/continuidad, (the) present/(el) presente.**

Build Fluency

Read aloud the following rhyme, and point out the words that sound alike. Return to the rhyme throughout the lesson to help develop vocabulary, sequencing skills, and lesson content.

How do communities change?
A **decade** goes by.
Some things change.
A **century** goes by.
More things change!

We tear down little stores
And build apartments with ten floors.
But hear us say,
"Some things stay the same way!"
Some things have **continuity**
In our community.

© Harcourt

Scaffolding the Content

Preview the Lesson

Tell students that all communities change. Have them recall ways they said their own community had changed, based on the photos they looked at earlier. Then have students look at pictures in the lesson. Encourage them to predict the kinds of changes the lesson will tell about.

• During **Teach**, pp. 156–159
• 30 minutes

Modify Instruction

Hand out the T-chart graphic organizer found on the blackline master page. Have students read the headings *Different* and *Same* with you, and remind them of their discussion of these ideas from Chapter 1.

1 **Over Time** Remind students that they have already talked about some ways that communities change. Have students look at the picture on page 157. Explain that this shows the city of Chicago in the past. Ask students to find ways the city is different from cities today. Tell them to draw these under the heading *Different.*

2 Explain that some things stay the same in cities, too. Tell students that when things stay the same, we say they have *continuity.* Call attention to the photo on page 156. Explain that it shows the city of Chicago today. Have students find things in the photo that show continuity. Ask them to draw or list those things under *Same* on their T-chart.

3 Tell students that buildings and other things in communities change. Point out that sometimes the kinds of work people do may change, too. Other times, the kinds of work people do stay the same. Ask questions to help students discover concrete examples. *Did workers use computers in the past? Do workers use horses to take people from place to place in the city now? Did workers build stores in the past? Do workers build stores now?* Have students write or make drawings on their T-charts to show how workers are the same and different over time.

4 **Changes Over Time** Point out that changes in a community can happen quickly or slowly. Tell students to look at the picture on page 158. Explain that it shows something that happened in Chicago in the past. Have students tell what happened, based on the picture. *Does the picture show a fast or slow change? What do you think people in the community did after the fire?*

5 Direct attention to the top picture on page 159. Explain that it shows a city called Jerome, Arizona. Tell students that Jerome was a very small city. Then people found a valuable metal called copper there. Lots of people moved to Jerome to dig up copper to sell. Explain that the city became small again after people stopped finding copper. Have students compare the two pictures, and draw on their chart other ways a community can change and stay the same.

Extend

Have students think about how their community might look in the future. Ask them to draw a picture showing what things they think might be the same and what things might be different.

• After **Teach**, pp. 156–159
• 15 minutes

Name _____ Date _____

How Do Communities Stay the Same?
How Do Communities Change?

Same	Different

Apply and Assess

Make a Brochure

Show examples of brochures. Point out pictures, headings, labels, and text. Explain to students that they will be making brochures to show ways their community has changed and ways it has stayed the same. Show them how to fold a sheet of paper to make a two-panel brochure. Have students copy the name of their community onto the cover panel. Encourage them to draw a cover picture. Inside, suggest that they show the past on one panel and the present on the other. Encourage them to use ideas they have already discussed about their community during the lesson.

• During **Close**, p. 159
• 20 minutes

- Allow beginning students to show continuity and change through pictures alone. Encourage them to dictate labels to you as they are able.
- Encourage intermediate students to write short captions for their drawings.
- Challenge advanced students to write a sentence or two under each drawing to explain what it shows.

Informal Lesson Assessment

	Beginning	Intermediate	Advanced
Task	Students draw pictures that show continuity and change in communities, and tell about their pictures.	Students draw pictures to show continuity and change in communities, and identify the changes with short phrases.	Students draw a picture of a community, and write sentences telling how the picture shows continuity and change.
Below Expectations	• drawings do not show continuity and change • student is unable to express ideas about the pictures verbally	• drawings do not show continuity and change • phrases do not relate to lesson concepts • spelling is invented	• drawing does not show both continuity and change • sentences do not relate to the concepts
Meets Expectations	• drawings show continuity and change • student expresses ideas about the pictures verbally	• drawings show continuity and change • phrases generally relate to lesson concepts • spelling is approximate	• drawing shows both continuity and change • sentences generally describe both concepts
Above Expectations	• drawings show continuity and change • student expresses ideas about the pictures in complete thoughts	• drawings show continuity and change • phrases specifically relate to concept • spelling is mostly correct	• drawing shows both continuity and change • sentences specifically identify examples of both concepts

© Harcourt

Build Background

Access Prior Knowledge

Discuss a problem, such as some students having trouble using the classroom computers. Ask: *How could we fix this problem? Who could fix the problem?* Point out that teachers and students can work together to solve problems. This makes their classroom better. Explain that people can also make their communities better.

• Before **Introduce**, p. 162
• 25 minutes

Lesson Vocabulary

Present the vocabulary using the same classroom problem. Explain that all students in your class have a **right** to use the computers. Different people having the same rights is called **equality.** Say: *We want to protect everyone's **civil rights.** Civil rights means rules and laws are the same for everyone. We want to make fair rules about the computers.* Have the class brainstorm ways to use the computers fairly. Tell them they will have a chance to vote on the best ideas. Students might think of an **invention** to help. Define the word. Point out that **engineers** are people who figure out how to make inventions work. Explain that the class might list lots of solutions. Students might make up sayings, or **slogans,** to tell why they like certain ideas. The class could **vote** to decide which ideas to use. Say: *Everyone in the class has the right to vote. The right to vote is called **suffrage.*** After introducing these ideas, revisit the questions from "Access Prior Knowledge," and encourage students to use the vocabulary to discuss them further.

Additional Vocabulary Model using context and pictures to help students understand the meanings of *flight* and *marches.* Present phrases such as *brought change to.* Have students use the words at the right, in sentences about familiar situations. Examples may include: *The new restaurant brought change to our community. Now, more people eat Thai food.* Use a similar approach to explain the other words and phrases in the margin.

Cognates As students read the lesson, you may wish to point out cognates such as: **invention/invención, canal/canal, locomotive/locomotora, vote/voto.**

brought change to
edges
elevator
flight (of stairs)
follow laws
free country
get (a message across)
marches
vote

Build Fluency

Read aloud the following rhyme, and point out the words that sound alike. Return to the chant throughout the lesson to help develop vocabulary, sequencing skills, and lesson content.

Communities change, change, change,
It's true, true, true!

People make buildings bigger, taller, stronger.
People make roads better, wider, longer.
Inventions make work faster and easier.
New ideas change the community, too.

People work for **civil rights, suffrage,** and **equality**
To make communities better for you and me.

© Harcourt

Scaffolding the Content

Preview the Lesson

Be sure students understand the concept of change. Show them a pile of books on a shelf. Have students watch as you organize the books. Say: *I changed the books on the shelf.* Explain that people also change their communities. Tell students they will learn many ways that people change their communities. Have them look at the headings and pictures to predict changes people make in communities.

• During **Teach**, pp. 162–167
• 30 minutes

Modify Instruction

Remind students of the classroom problem they discussed at the beginning of the lesson. Tell students they will use a *Why, What, Who* chart to make notes about changes the lesson tells about.

1 **Building Outward** Explain that one way people change their communities is by building roads. Ask: *Why do people build roads?* People also build canals. Point out that canals are like water roads. People use boats to travel on them. Tell students that one person who helped people get from place to place was George Stephenson. Over 150 years ago, he invented a locomotive, a train engine that ran on a track. The locomotive connected communities. Point out the pictures on pages 162 and 163. Ask students to add to their chart some ideas about changes from this part of the lesson.

2 **Building Upward** Tell students that people also change their communities by making new buildings. Ask: *Why do people need buildings?* William Jennings used steel and iron to make taller buildings than anyone had before. Point out and discuss the tall buildings on page 164. Then Elisha Otis invented elevators to help people go up and down in tall buildings. Tell students to summarize these changes on their chart.

3 **Workers for Suffrage** Point out that sometimes people change *things* in their community. Other times, people change *ideas* in their community. Tell students that over 100 years ago, women could not vote. They could not choose leaders and laws for our country. Ask: *Does this sound fair?* Susan B. Anthony and Elizabeth Cady *thought this was wrong, too. They helped make a change so that women could vote.*

4 **Workers for Equality** Explain that Mohandas Gandhi was another person who changed ideas. He lived in India. He believed people in his country should have freedom. He worked to make that change. Dr. Martin Luther King, Jr. changed ideas in our country. He worked to be sure all people were treated fairly. Provide time for students to review these ideas on their chart.

Extend

Have students think about physical changes in their school, such as new library books or a newly painted area. Then have them think about changes in ideas or in how things are done, such as changing lunch times. Ask each student to draw one change. Assemble the drawings into a book called "People Change Schools."

• After **Teach**, pp. 162–167
• 15 minutes

How Do People Change Their Communities?
Why Do People Change Their Communities?

What?	Why?	Who?
_____	_____	_____
_____	_____	_____
_____	_____	_____
_____	_____	_____
_____	_____	_____
_____	_____	_____
_____	_____	_____
_____	_____	_____
_____	_____	_____
_____	_____	_____
_____	_____	_____
_____	_____	_____
_____	_____	_____

School-Home Connection Have students take this page home to share with their families. They can use the information on the chart to tell their families about how and why people change their communities.

Apply and Assess

Write a Paragraph

Have students revisit their *Why, What, Who* charts. Ask them to choose information they wrote about a particular person for the focus of their paragraph. Ask: *What is most important about this person?*

• During **Close**, p. 167
• 20 minutes

- Have beginning students draw a sequence chain about their chosen subject. Have them label the events in the sequence chain to share details as they are able.
- Provide sentence frames for intermediate students to use to write their paragraphs.
- Challenge advanced students to begin their paragraphs with a topic sentence, to use sequence words such as *first, next,* and *last* in presenting details, and to end with a conclusion sentence.

Informal Lesson Assessment

	Beginning	Intermediate	Advanced
Task	Student draws and labels pictures showing ways people change their communities.	Student draws pictures showing ways people change communities and writes phrases to explain the drawings.	Student makes a list of sentences that tell different ways people change communities.
Below Expectations	• drawings do not show ways people change communities • student cannot use words to tell about the drawings	• phrases do not clearly connect to drawings • spelling is invented	• writing does not clearly relate ways people change communities • thoughts not in sentence form
Meets Expectations	• drawings show a few ways people change communities • student is able to say words to tell about the drawings	• phrases generally tell about a few ways people change communities • spelling is approximate	• sentences generally relate how people change communities • most sentences are complete thoughts with capitals and end punctuation
Above Expectations	• drawings show several ways people change communities • student is able to say phrases and simple sentences about the drawings	• phrases specifically address ways people change communities • most of the spelling is correct	• sentences specifically relate how people change communities • all sentences are complete thoughts with capitals and end punctuation

© Harcourt

Build Background

Access Prior Knowledge

Remind students that an invention is something made for the first time that helps people do something. Provide such examples as the stapler, which helps people put together pieces of paper. Have students work together to list other inventions used in the classroom.

• Before **Introduce**, p. 170
• 20 minutes

Lesson Vocabulary

Write **technology** on the board. Pronounce the word, and explain that it means tools and machines that make our life easier. Ask each student to write the word on a sticky note, and attach it to an example of technology in the classroom. Encourage students to explain, or show, how these forms of technology help them in their daily lives.

Additional Vocabulary While students will likely know the adjective *good*, they may not know the word *goods*. Explain that *goods* are things that are bought and sold. Ask: *What* goods *do you buy in a grocery store? In a toy store?* Be sure that students understand the broader definition of *tool*. Explain that hammers and saws are tools, but so are forks, brooms, and pencils. Invite students to think of other tools. Preteach the phrase *led to* by asking questions, such as: *What* led to *our opening the window?* Teach *on their own* by having students identify things they are allowed to do on their own. Review other words in the margin in the context of the lesson, and have students make their own sentences.

afford	goods
causing	led to
code	on their own
communicate	tool

Cognates As students read the lesson, you may wish to point out cognates such as: **technology/tecnología, telegraph/telégrafo, telephone/teléfono, automobile/automóvil, airplane/aeroplano, electricity/electricidad.**

Build Fluency

Read aloud the following rhyme, and point out the words that sound alike. Return to the rhyme throughout the lesson to help develop vocabulary, sequencing skills, and lesson content.

Technology is really great.
It helps people communicate.
Inventions like the telegraph and telephone
Keep people from feeling all alone.

Technology is really great.
It keeps us from being late.
Take a train or plane or car
If you need to travel far.

Technology is really great.
It helps put food on our plates.
Aren't you glad that long ago
Someone invented the stove and radio?

© Harcourt

Scaffolding the Content

Preview the Lesson

Have students look at the heading "Changes in Communication." Ask: *What inventions do you think this part of the lesson may tell about?* Encourage students to use the pictures as well as prior knowledge to respond. Continue with the headings "Changes in Transportation" and "Changes in the Home." Tell students that they will learn about inventions that are examples of each kind of change.

• During **Teach**, pp. 170–175
• 30 minutes

Modify Instruction

Remind students of award shows they have seen on television, or school awards assemblies. Tell them that they will pretend to be invention judges. They will learn about some inventions, and decide which they think are most important. Tell students to take notes on the web handout to help them remember the inventions the class discusses.

1 Communication Ask students to tell, or act out, the sequence of events of mailing and receiving a letter. Have them look at the picture on page 170. Explain that long ago, riders on horses delivered the mail. Write the following on the board. a = • -   p = • - - •   t = -   Explain that this is a code people used to send messages. People used it to send messages over wires. It is called the telegraph. Explain that the next important communication invention was the telephone. It was invented by Alexander Graham Bell. Have students notice similarities and differences among the telephones on page 171. Provide time for students to record ideas on the appropriate branch of their web.

2 Transportation Tell them that the next important transportation invention was the automobile, or car. Explain that at first, cars cost a lot of money. Most people could not buy them. Then Henry Ford found a way to make cars that cost less. Have students look at the picture on page 172. Ask them to compare cars and roads of long ago to those of today. Tell students that another important invention was the airplane. Ask students what words they would use to describe the airplane on page 173. Provide time for students to record transportation changes on their webs.

3 Home Explain the role of Thomas Edison and Lewis Latimer in inventing the electric light bulb. Point out that other inventions use electricity. Have students name inventions in their classroom and home that use electricity. Ask students to record important ideas on their webs. Say: *Remember that you are pretending to be judges. Which inventions do you think are most important? Draw a star next to them.* Ask students to share and explain their responses.

Extend

Divide the class into groups. Assign each group to focus on either communication, transportation, or home. Have groups pretend to be inventors trying to think of new ideas for the future. Ask students to draw pictures of technology they might use in the future.

• After **Teach**, pp. 170–175
• 20 minutes

© Harcourt

Name _____ Date _____

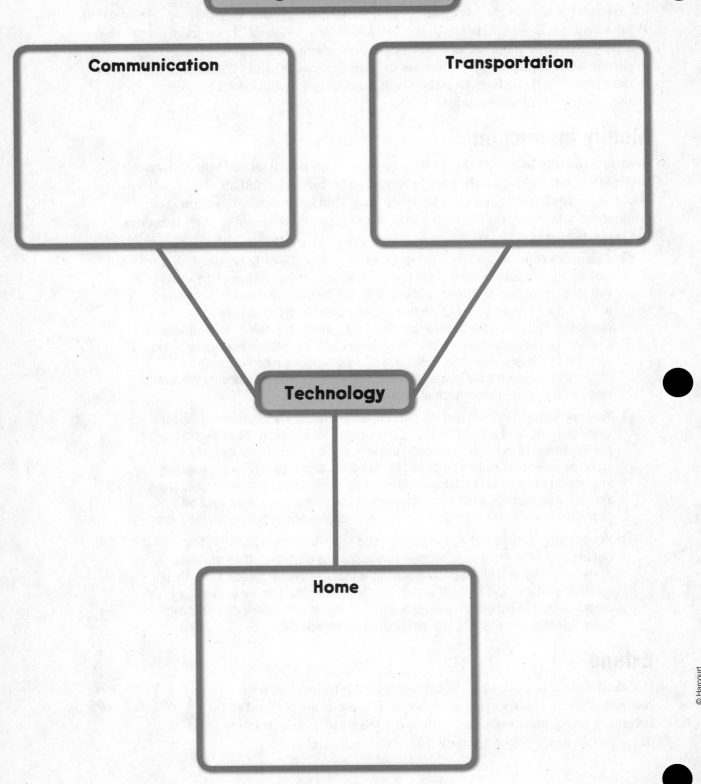

Changes in Technology

Communication

Transportation

Technology

Home

© Harcourt

Apply and Assess

Make a Chart

Show students how to draw a two-column chart. Demonstrate making column headings for "Inventor" and "Invention." Use your finger to demonstrate how to scan down page 171 while looking for the name of an inventor. When you come to *Samuel Morse,* model copying the name from the text. Then use a think-aloud to show students how to find information for the other column. *I see the photo of Samuel Morse at the top of the page. I remember that his invention used a secret code. The code had dots and dashes instead of letters. I cannot remember the name of the invention. I will look at the heading. It says:* Samuel Morse and the Telegraph. *The name of the invention is the telegraph. I will write that on my chart.* Have students use the techniques you demonstrated to complete their charts.

- During **Close**, p. 175
- 15 minutes

- Write the names of inventors on the board in a word box for beginning students. Tell students to use the box to help them spell the names. Let them draw the inventions.

- Have intermediate students exchange papers and check each other's ideas and spelling against the text.

- Encourage advanced students to add a column telling why each invention changed people's lives.

Informal Lesson Assessment

	Beginning	Intermediate	Advanced
Task	Students draw and label pictures showing different kinds of important inventions.	Students make a list of important inventions sorted into categories.	Students write a summary of important inventions in each category.
Below Expectations	• pictures are not relevant to the topic • student is unable to label pictures	• list is irrelevant to topic • student can read list	• summary is overly general or irrelevant • items are not discussed in categories
Meets Expectations	• pictures are relevant • student can name each invention pictured	• list of inventions relevant to all categories • inventions are correctly categorized	• summary identifies several specific inventions • inventions are grouped into categories
Above Expectations	• pictures represent communication, transportation, and home • student correctly identifies each invention	• list of all inventions from the text • headings are used to categorize the items	• summary identifies all inventions discussed in the text • topic sentences or headings are used to indicate categories

© Harcourt

Build Background

Access Prior Knowledge

Gather such classroom items as paper, pencils, and a calculator. Have students discuss which items they think were invented a short time ago and which may have been used for a long time. Encourage students to tell reasons for their responses. Tell students they will learn about some very old inventions and their inventors.

• Before **Introduce**, p. 178
• 30 minutes

Lesson Vocabulary

Introduce the words by discussing their relationship to each other. Write the following word pair on the board: *ancient/modern.* Discuss with students the meanings of the words. Ask: *Are they the same or opposite? Why?* Then write: *civilization/empire.* Explain that a civilization is a large group of people living together. The people in a civilization have their own culture and rules. Then point out that an empire is all the land and people that one strong nation rules. Ask: *How might the words* civilization *and* empire *be connected?* Continue to present meanings, and discuss relationships between the following word pairs: **democracy/republic, trade/port.**

Additional Vocabulary As you encounter the words *record* and *stands* in the reading, explain the multiple meanings of the words. Also, be sure students understand phrases such as: *by hand.* Demonstrate writing by hand and writing with a computer, and use the phrase. Use demonstrations or context to clarify the meanings of the other phrases in the margin.

by hand	record
fireworks	stands
keep track of	take part in
known for	well organized
pulleys	wheeled cart

Cognates As students read the lesson, you may wish to point out cognates such as: **civilization/civilización, modern/moderno, democracy/democracia, republic/república.**

Build Fluency

Read aloud the following rhyme, and point out the words that sound alike. Return to the rhyme throughout the lesson to help develop vocabulary, sequencing skills, and lesson content.

Was the United States the first of many nations? No! Before us there were **ancient civilizations.**

There was Rome, Mali, Egypt, Mesopotamia, and Greece. These **empires** had ideas about how to live in peace.

They set up **republics** and **democracies** so people got along.

Today, **modern** civilizations use these ideas to stay strong.

Don't you think that it is exciting That ancient civilizations invented paper, fireworks, and writing?

© Harcourt

Scaffolding the Content

Preview the Lesson

Call attention to the maps in the lesson. Tell students that the maps show ancient communities. Explain that the lesson tells about important ideas from each place. Help students write the names for the communities on sticky notes, and place them on a world map so they may see their locations relative to each other and to the United States.

• During **Teach**, pp. 178–185
• 30 minutes

Modify Instruction

Tell students that they will learn about civilizations from long, long ago. Pass out copies of the blackline master on the next page. Explain that students will draw or list ideas from each civilization that we still use today. Give students time to take notes.

1 **Ancient Mesopotamia** Have students repeat *Mesopotamia* after you. Explain that this civilization was one of the oldest in the world. One city was called Sumer. Point out that the people in Sumer invented carts with wheels. Ask: *Why was this an important invention?* Explain that they also invented writing. Ask: *How would your life be different if we did not have writing?*

2 **Ancient Egypt** Call attention to the picture of the pyramid on page 180. Explain that ancient Egyptian kings and queens were buried in pyramids. Tell students that workers did not have trucks, tractors, or earthmovers. They used wheels, pulleys, and ramps to move big blocks of stone. Ask: *How do we use those tools today?*

3 **Ancient China** Explain that people in ancient China invented paper. Ask: *How many uses can you name for paper?* Tell students to pretend they live in ancient times. Say: *Pretend that you wrote something and want to give a copy to six friends. You would have to copy it six times.* Explain that the Chinese invented a way to copy pages by making a print of them.

4 **Ancient Greece** Tell students that Athens was an important city in ancient Greece. It was important because it was the first democracy. The United States is a modern democracy. Greece also had many famous artists, builders, and writers. Ask: *What does the picture at the bottom of page 182 show about Greece?*

5 **Ancient Rome** Ancient Rome was where Italy is today. The civilization is important because it had the first republic. A republic is a government where people vote for leaders, and the leaders make laws.

6 **Mali** Tell students that Mali was a rich empire. People came there to trade gold for salt and cloth.

Extend

Have students look at nonfiction picture books about ancient civilizations. Ask them to find pictures of things those civilizations invented. Provide time for students to share what they learn.

• After **Teach**, pp. 178–185
• 15 minutes

Name _____

Date _____

China

Greece

Mesopotamia

Rome

Egypt

Mali

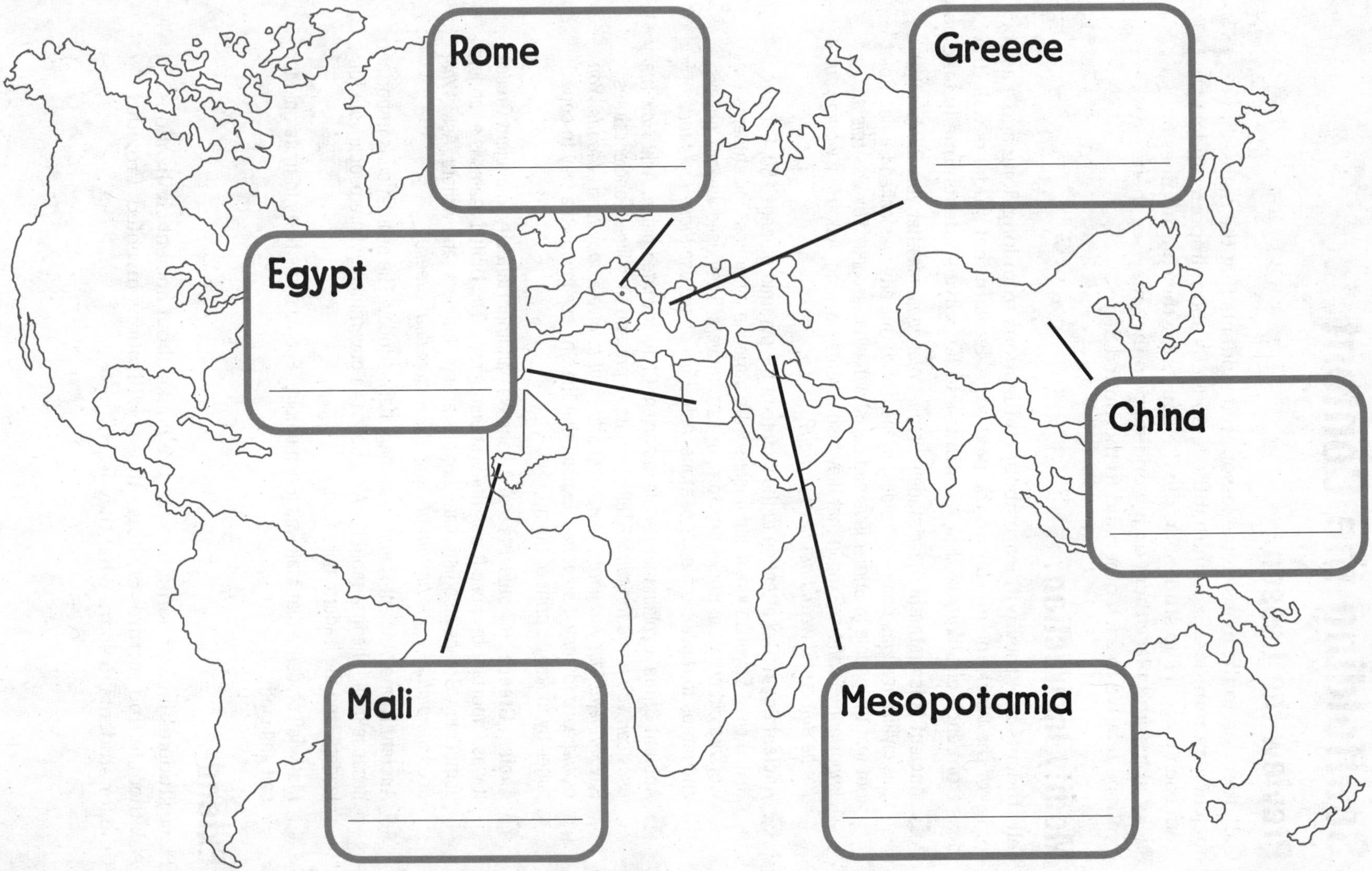

© Harcourt

School-Home Connection Have students take this page home to share with their families. They can use the information on the map to tell their families about ideas that come from ancient communities.

Apply and Assess

Create a Radio Interview

Have students use oral rehearsal as a prewriting activity. Pretend to be a person from ancient Mesopotamia. Show the class your new invention. Say: *Look! I just had a new idea. It is a cart. It has wheels on it. What questions do you have about my cart?* Encourage students to ask questions. *(What do you use it for? How did you think of it? Why did you make it?)* Then have pairs of students follow your model. Tell them to select a civilization and an idea.

• During **Close**, p. 185
• 30 minutes

One student pretends to be the inventor. The other student asks questions about the invention. Suggest that they take notes of their conversation to use when writing their interview.

- For beginning students, brainstorm a list of simple questions, including the ones you used in modeling, that can be used with various ideas and innovations.

- Tell intermediate students to rehearse their interviews several times before tape-recording them. Have students help each other with names of civilizations.

- Explain to advanced students that they should think of questions that cannot be answered with *yes* or *no.* This will make their interviews more interesting. Provide examples, such as questions that begin with *why* and *how.*

Informal Lesson Assessment

	Beginning	Intermediate	Advanced
Task	Students draw pictures of ideas from ancient civilizations that we still use today, and name the civilizations.	Students make a chart showing ideas from ancient civilizations that we still use today.	Students write a sentence about each ancient civilization that tells which of its ideas we still use today.
Below Expectations	• drawings are irrelevant • cannot name ancient civilizations	• items on chart are irrelevant • items are not correctly matched with civilizations	• response is irrelevant • ideas not in sentence form
Meets Expectations	• drawings show a few ideas from ancient civilizations • correctly matches most ideas and civilizations	• identifies as least one idea related to each civilization in the text • correctly matches most ideas with the related civilization	• identifies at least one idea with each civilization • most responses express complete thoughts
Above Expectations	• draws ideas from each civilization in the text • correctly identifies the source of each idea	• charts all the inventions • correctly matches all inventions with civilizations	• identifies several ideas with each civilization • all responses are complete sentences

Build Background

Access Prior Knowledge

Students who have recently come to the United States may have little knowledge of Native Americans. Provide picture books about Native Americans of the past and today. Allow students to browse through those books to build background about Native American cultures. Explain that Native Americans made our first communities. Encourage questions.

• Before **Introduce**, p. 190
• 30 minutes

Lesson Vocabulary

Write *tribe* on the board. Explain that people in a tribe share land and ways of life. Ask: *How is a family like a tribe? How is it different? How is a class like a tribe? How is it different? What other groups are like tribes?* Next, write *language* on the board, and define the word. Have students identify different languages they know, and make a class list. Next, ask students tell about special class events that have happened so far in the school year. Explain that they are sharing their **oral history.** Finally, define the word **shelter.** Then show or draw various pictures such as a house, a car, a tent, a doghouse, and a hat. Ask students to determine which are examples of shelter. Explain that students will learn how these words relate to Native Americans.

Additional Vocabulary Have students tell the meanings they know for *bark* and *squash*. If they are not familiar with the meanings as used in the lesson, explain them in advance. Then be sure students understand the concept of *meeting one's needs*. Ask questions, such as: *How can you meet your need for food? How can you meet your need for a quiet place to read?* Also introduce the phrase *way of life*, using common or familiar experiences. Review other words in the margin in the context of the lesson, and have students make their own sentences.

bark	poles
crops	protects
(animal) hide	squash
meet needs	store (v.)
nearby	way of life

Cognates As students read the lesson, you may wish to point out cognates such as: **tribe/tribu, buffalo/búfalo.**

Build Fluency

Read aloud the following rhyme, and point out the words that sound alike. Return to the rhyme throughout the lesson to help develop vocabulary, sequence skills, and lesson content.

Native Americans were the first people to live on this land.
They lived in groups called **tribes,** or bands.
The life of Native Americans is not a mystery.
We know a lot about it from **oral history.**
They made **shelters** of clay bricks, wood, or hide.
They built them with Native American pride.
Native Americans had to hunt, gather, and grow
Foods like fish, berries, corn, and buffalo.

© Harcourt

Scaffolding the Content

Preview the Lesson

Give each student an index card labeled *Who, What, When, Where, How,* or *Why.* Have them browse the lesson, noting pictures and headings. Ask students to make up questions about Native Americans using the words on their cards. Tell students that they will look for answers in the lesson.

• During **Teach**, pp. 190–193
• 30 minutes

Modify Instruction

Have students look at the questions on the question web handout. Ask them to add their question from "Preview the Lesson" on the sixth blank branch. Tell students to listen for the answers to the questions as they discuss the lesson.

1 The First People Explain that the first communities in our country began long ago, and the people who started them were Native Americans. Explain that there were many groups, or tribes, of Native Americans. Each tribe had its own language and way of life. Have students look at the picture on page 190. Ask students to describe how the Ute father and son are dressed. Pause for students to add details to their webs.

2 Where Native Americans Lived Tell students that Native Americans lived in all parts of North America. Have students look at the map on page 191 and identify places Native Americans lived. Point to the East on the map. Tell students that there were forests and rivers in that area. Ask: *How do you think people in these communities used the forests? How do you think they used the rivers?* Indicate the Southwest. Tell students that this part of the country is hot and dry. Explain that Native Americans there learned to farm. Point out that they made homes of clay bricks. Ask: *Why do you think they built that kind of home?* Point to the Northwest. Tell students that people there used resources from forests, rivers, and oceans. Allow time for students to use this information to answer questions on their webs.

3 Hunting Communities Explain that people in some early communities hunted animals for food. Point to the Great Plains. Explain that Native Americans who lived there hunted for buffalo. Say: *Find a picture of a buffalo on page 192.* Point out that they used the meat for food. They used the bones to make tools. They used the skin to make clothing and shelters. They followed groups of buffalo to hunt them. Point to a tepee on the page. Ask: *Why do you think the hunters used this kind of home?* Have students add to their webs.

4 Farming Communities Point out that some Native Americans later stopped moving from place to place. They started to stay in one place and plant food. Some things they grew were corn, beans, and squash. Some built longhouses like the one on page 193. Ask: *How is a longhouse different from a tepee?* Ask students to add final notes to their webs.

Extend

Ask students to look at the question on the sixth branch of their webs. Ask: *Did you find the answer?* If not, have students use books, bookmarked sites on the Internet about Native Americans, and other resources to answer the question. Also, have them use those resources to add to the other parts of their webs.

• After **Teach**, pp. 190–193
• 20 minutes

© Harcourt

Who started our first communities?

_____

_____

Where did our first communities start?

_____

_____

When did our first communities start?

_____

_____

Our First Communities

What natural resources did Native Americans have?

_____

_____

How did Native Americans live?

_____

_____

My question:

_____

_____

School-Home Connection Have students take this page home to share with their families. They can use the information on the web to tell about Native American communities.

Apply and Assess

Make a Map

Have students revisit the map on page 191. Point to each part of the map, such as the title, locations, and so on. Talk with students about the purpose of each part. Have students notice how the map maker indicates places where Native Americans lived. Share information about where Native Americans lived in your community or state. Discuss students' ideas about how to show this information on a map. *How will your map be like the one on page 191? How will your map be different?*

• During **Close**, p. 193
• 20 minutes

- Give groups of beginning students large outline maps of your community or state. Have them collaborate on making maps. Write words on index cards that they may copy onto their maps.

- Have intermediate students brainstorm words they may need to write in making their maps. Write these on chart paper, and display the list for their reference.

- Ask advanced students to write a few sentence captions under their map to summarize what it shows.

Informal Lesson Assessment

	Beginning	Intermediate	Advanced
Task	Ask: *Who formed the first communities?* Students act out, or use single words to describe details about the life of Native Americans.	Students respond in writing to: *Who formed the first communities? How did they live?*	Students write a conversation between two Native Americans from different areas, and include different ways of life in their conversation.
Below Expectations	• cannot respond to the question • situations acted out, or words used are not relevant	• cannot respond to questions • minimal response with single words such as: *hunt, tepee*	• writes irrelevant or overly general conversation • uses a different format such as an explanatory paragraph
Meets Expectations	• correctly responds to the question • acts out, or uses one-word descriptions of aspects of Native American life	• correctly responds to questions • uses phrases or simple sentences to identify a few characteristics of Native American life	• writes about a few different aspects of Native American life • writes in the form of a conversation between two people
Above Expectations	• correctly responds to the question • uses vivid words to describe Native American life	• correctly responds to questions • uses simple sentences to describe aspects of Native American life	• writes about several aspects of Native American life

Build Background

Access Prior Knowledge

Call attention to the picture on page 196. If possible, show other pictures of
Columbus as a sailor and explorer. Ask students to share what they know
about him. Ask: *What did he do? Why is he important?* Tell students they
will learn more about Columbus and others who came to the place we call
the Americas.

• Before **Introduce**, p. 196
• 25 minutes

Lesson Vocabulary

Write *explorer* on the board. Ask: *What do you think this means? Do you think explorers
need to be brave? Explain.* Then write *settle* on the board. Explain that it means "to
stay in a place." Write *settlement* and *settler.* Explain that one reason settlers go to a
place is to **claim** land. Tell students that claiming is saying something belongs to
you. Say: *I claim this desk.* Have students show items such as pencils and notebooks
that they claim as their own. Point out that another reason settlers go to a place is to
be free to follow their **religion.** Explain that a religion is something people believe
in. Ask students to name religions that they know. Tell students that settlers and the
people already living in a place may not get along. They may fight, or have a
conflict. Ask: *What may people have a conflict about?* Say: *One thing people had a conflict
about many years ago was* **slavery.** *Slavery means one person owns another
person. The owner makes the other person work with no pay.* Ask: *How do you
think a person felt about someone forcing them to work for no pay? Why?*

Additional Vocabulary Help students use context and prior knowledge to
understand the meaning of the words and phrases in the margin as they
encounter them in the lesson.

Cognates As students read the lesson, you may wish to point out
cognates such as: **explorer/explorador, religion/religión, conflict/
conflicto.**

continent
enslave
follow (a religion)
heritage
maintain peace
reach
spread (religion)
stepson
(fur-)trading post
treasure

Build Fluency

Read aloud the following rhyme,
and point out the words that sound
alike. Return to the rhyme
throughout the lesson to help
develop vocabulary, sequence skills,
and lesson content.

In 1492, **explorer** Christopher Columbus took a trip.
He left Spain to find Asia in his sailing ship.
Columbus found the Americas instead, you know.
Soon, people from France and England also wanted
to go.
Settlers from many countries came to **claim** land.
They built houses, cabins, and churches by hand.
Some settlers came for freedom to pray.
Some brought in slaves to work all day.
They built Jamestown and Plymouth by the sea
So people from around the world could be free.

© Harcourt

Scaffolding the Content

Preview the Lesson

Have students look at the pictures of settlements on pages 197, 198, and 200. Ask: *Are these pictures of long ago or now? How do you know? What is the same about the communities? What is different?* Tell students they will learn about these old settlements. They will learn who helped start them.

• During **Teach**, pp. 196–203
• 30 minutes

Modify Instruction

Distribute the Sequence Steps blackline master. Have students notice the dates. Tell them that they will find out what happened on those dates.

1 **Exploring North America** 1492: Tell students that Columbus left the country of Spain in 1492. He wanted to find a new way to get to Asia. Instead, he reached the place we now call the Americas. (Help students find Spain, Asia, and the Americas on a map.) Then explorers from other countries came to the Americas. Some came to claim land for their countries. Some came to tell others about their religions. Provide time for students to make an entry on their Sequence Steps for 1492.

1565: Tell students that Pedro Menéndez de Avilés came from Spain to the place we now call Florida. He started the town of St. Augustine. Then, other Spanish explorers came. They claimed land in South America and North America. (Help students find the areas on the map.) Ask students to write a note for 1565 on their Sequence Steps.

2 **A French Settlement** 1763: Explain that Pierre Laclède and Renè Chouteau were from France. They explored the Mississippi River. They stopped at the place we call St. Louis. They started a fur-trading business. (Help students locate France, the Mississippi, and St. Louis on a map.) Have students add to their Sequence Steps.

3 **An English Settlement** 1607: Tell students that a ship full of men and boys came from England. They came to the place we now call Virginia. They hoped to find gold. They named their community Jamestown. (Locate England, Virginia, and Jamestown on the map.) Then some settlers argued with the Native Americans who already lived there. Their leader, John Smith, helped them learn to be peaceful. Have students fill in the lines for 1607.

1612: Point out that settler John Rolfe started to grow tobacco in Jamestown. Then the community needed more workers. In 1619, the settlers started to make people from Africa come to the Americas to work. They made them work for no pay. This was slavery. Have students make entries on their Sequence Steps.

4 **Another English Settlement** 1620: Explain that a ship called the Mayflower came from England. It stopped at the place we now call Massachusetts. (Help students find Massachusetts on a map.) The people on the ship wanted to be free to follow their religion. Then they started a community called Plymouth. Have students record these ideas on their Sequence Steps.

Extend

Have students add to the events on their Sequence Steps. Ask them to write *Then* and tell something else that happened after the event they noted under each date. For example, *Columbus came to the Americas. Then explorers from other countries came.*

• After **Teach**, pp. 196–203
• 15 minutes

1492 _____
_____

1565 _____
_____

1607 _____
_____

1612 _____
_____

1619 _____
_____

1620 _____
_____

1763 _____
_____

 School-Home Connection Have students take this page home to share with their families. They can use the information on the steps to tell their families about people from Europe who started communities in the Americas.

© Harcourt

Apply and Assess

Make a Chart

• During **Close**, p. 203
• 20 minutes

Remind students of their "Preview the Lesson" discussion of the settlements on pages 197, 198, and 200. Help them recall similarities and differences they noticed in the pictures. Point out that they learned more about these places from the text. Encourage students to talk about additional similarities and differences. Then have students select two of the three settlements to use to make a chart. Show them how to set up a T-chart with two settlement names above the *T*. Have students list details about each settlement in the columns.

- Allow beginning students to use pictures and words on their chart. Help them share their work by asking *yes/no* questions about their chart.

- Encourage intermediate students to use phrases on their chart. Provide time for them to share and elaborate on the notes on their chart.

- Permit advanced students to share their T-charts. Then encourage them to make a summary statement telling whether they think the two settlements they compared are more alike or different. Ask presenters to use details on their chart to back up their conclusion.

Informal Lesson Assessment

	Beginning	Intermediate	Advanced
Task	Students draw a community in North America that people from Europe settled. They tell about their drawing.	Students write a phrase or simple sentence about each of the following: a French settlement, a Spanish settlement, an English settlement.	Students write a short narrative as an explorer from Europe, telling about the experience of starting a community in North America.
Below Expectations	• drawing is irrelevant • cannot verbally tell about the drawing	• writing is irrelevant or incorrect	• narrative is irrelevant or overly general
Meets Expectations	• drawing addresses the topic • cannot verbally tell about the drawing	• writing tells at least one fact about each type of settlement • phrases and at least a couple of simple sentences are used	• writing gives general information about a European settlement • minimal supporting details are included
Above Expectations	• drawing shows details of an early community • uses words and phrases to tell about what the drawing shows	• writing tells more than one fact about each type of settlement • most information is in simple sentence format	• writing provides sufficient detail taken from the text and pictures in the lesson • narrative form is correctly used

Build Background

Access Prior Knowledge

Students may not be familiar with John Adams, Benjamin Franklin, Thomas Jefferson, and George Washington. Show a picture of each person, and tell why he is important. Then ask each student to pretend to be one of the figures. Have them tell something about themselves without saying the person's name. Ask the class to guess who the student is pretending to be.

• Before **Introduce**, p. 204
• 25 minutes

Lesson Vocabulary

Give each student a large sticky note with a vocabulary word on it. Have students look up the meanings. Then, put the following sentences on sentence strips. Read them aloud and have students place their words on the appropriate sentences. *1. The toy cost five dollars plus twenty-five cents _____. (tax) 2. The _____ of Virginia was ruled by England. (colony) 3. A _____ helps people set up a government. (constitution) 4. The leader of our country is our _____. (president) 5. We have the _____ to decide on our laws. (freedom) 6. Telling things you like about your country is a way to show _____. (patriotism) 7. Sometimes people have to fight for their _____. (independence) 8. Countries set up new governments after a _____. (revolution)*

Additional Vocabulary Review the words or phrases in the margin in the context of the lesson, and have students make their own sentences.

Cognates As students read the lesson, you may wish to point out cognates such as: **colony/colonia, revolution/revolución, independence/independencia, constitution/constitución, patriotism/patriotismo, president/presidente.**

approve	ruled by
found	throw away
mind	train
part	would rather
reach	

Build Fluency

Read aloud the following rhyme, and point out the words that sound alike. Return to the rhyme throughout the lesson to help develop vocabulary, sequence skills, and lesson content.

The North American **colonies** belonged to England, far away.
At first, everything worked out OK.
Then England passed laws that were unfair.
The colonists were angry, but England didn't care.
Colonists did not want to pay **taxes** on sugar and tea.
They showed their anger by dumping the tea into the sea.
Next, they thought it would make sense
To declare their **freedom** and fight for **independence.**
But England did not agree
With the colonists' wish to be free.
So the colonists' only solution
Was a long, hard **revolution.**
American soldiers fought to be free.
That made life better for you and me.

© Harcourt

Scaffolding the Content

● Preview the Lesson

Explain that this lesson tells how people fought for freedom and founded, or began, the United States. Have students look at the headings and pictures for each section. Ask them to think of a question they think each section will answer. Record the questions on the board. After studying the lesson, revisit the list to see which questions students are able to answer.

• During **Teach**, pp. 204–209
• 30 minutes

Modify Instruction

Tell students that you want them to pretend to be news reporters during the 1700s. Explain that the lesson will talk about that time in history. They will write about important things that happened. Distribute copies of the blackline master on the next page.

❶ Freedom from England Explain that in the 1700s, there were 13 English settlements, or colonies, in North America. The colonies belonged to England. At first, the colonists were happy. Later, they were not happy. England started to make laws that the colonists did not like. The laws said the colonists had to pay extra money, or taxes, for things like tea and sugar from England. The colonists did not think the laws were fair. They were not allowed to help make up the laws, but they had to obey them. Ask: *How would this make you feel?* Tell students that one day, the colonists got very angry. They went to the harbor in Boston. They threw all the English tea off a ship into the water. We call this the Boston Tea Party. (Discuss with students the picture on page 204.) That made England angry. Explain that in 1775, a war started between the colonists and England.

❷ A Declaration is Made Tell students that leaders from the colonies met in 1776. The leaders were John Adams, Benjamin Franklin, Thomas Jefferson, and others. (Lead students in discussing the picture on page 206.) They wrote an important paper. We call this paper the Declaration of Independence. The paper said that the colonies did not want to belong to England. It said they wanted to start their own country. This was the beginning of the United States of America.

The war that started in 1775 was still going on. George Washington was the leader of the American army. They did not have many things they needed. (Discuss the pictures on page 207.) The soldiers were very brave, however. They fought hard and won the war in 1783. The colonies were free. They became their own country.

❸ New Laws Are Made The new country needed a government. It needed a set of laws. The leaders of the new country met in Philadelphia to talk about the government. They said they wanted to be sure people had rights. In 1789, the leaders agreed on a set of laws. The set of laws is called the Constitution of the United States.

Have students retell what they have learned, revisit the pictures in the lesson, and then respond to the headlines handout.

Extend

Have small groups work together to share their newspaper articles for a particular date. Ask them to use the ideas they have shared to write a skit about the historical event on that day. Provide time for groups to perform their skits.

• After **Teach**, pp. 204–209
• 30 minutes

© Harcourt

Name _____ Date _____

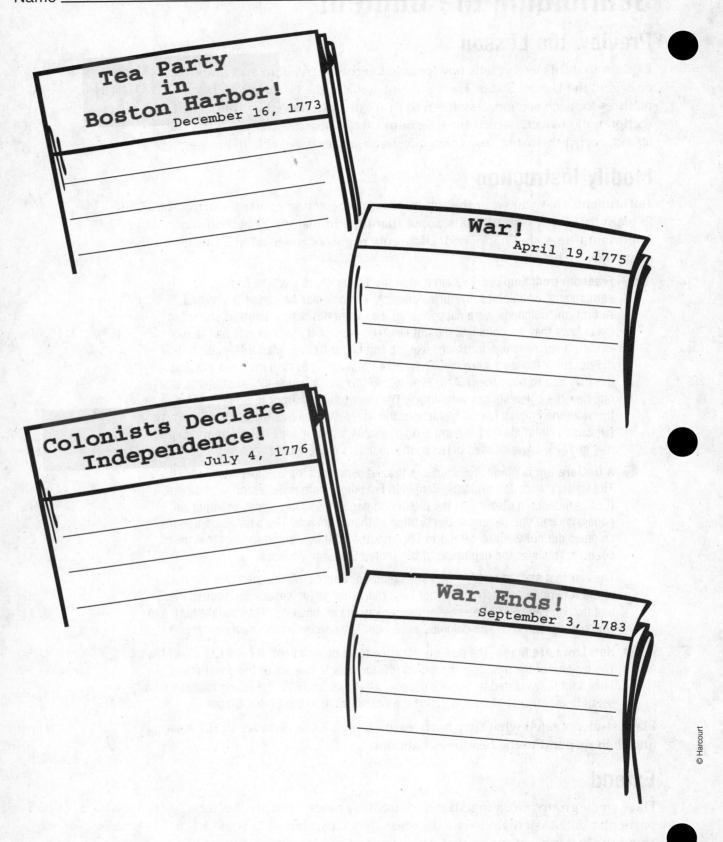

Tea Party in Boston Harbor!
December 16, 1773

War!
April 19, 1775

Colonists Declare Independence!
July 4, 1776

War Ends!
September 3, 1783

School-Home Connection Have students take this page home to share with their families. They can use their newspaper articles to tell how the colonists won their freedom from England.

© Harcourt

Apply and Assess

Make a Time Line

Have students revisit pages 160–161 to recall what they learned about time lines. Ask: *Why do we make time lines? What are the important parts of a time line?* Have students review the lesson to decide what dates to put on their time lines. List the dates on the board, and have students tell what is important about each date. Then have them use the listed dates and ideas from the discussion to create a time line. Suggest that they may also use their blackline master as a resource for this task.

• During **Close**, p. 209
• 20 minutes

- Beginning students may make an illustrated time line. Provide time for them to share their work, and tell about the pictures as they are able.

- Have intermediate students use phrases to tell about important events. Allow them to share their time lines, and elaborate on what they have written.

- Ask advanced students to begin their paragraphs with a topic sentence, use sequence words such as *first, next,* and *at last* in presenting details, and end with a conclusion sentence.

Informal Lesson Assessment

	Beginning	**Intermediate**	**Advanced**
Task	Students create a labeled and illustrated sequence chain to show how people fought for freedom in the United States.	Students write sentences telling how people fought for freedom in the United States.	Students write a paragraph summarizing how people fought for freedom in the United States.
Below Expectations	• pictures and labels do not relate to lesson content • pictures and labels are not in sequential order	• sentences are irrelevant to the lesson • events are not in sequential order	• writing does not address lesson content • events are out of order • response is not in paragraph form
Meets Expectations	• pictures and labels tell most major events from the lesson • events are in sequential order	• sentences tell most major events from the lesson • events are in sequential order	• writing addresses most major events from the lesson • information is in paragraph form
Above Expectations	• pictures and labels address all major events in the lesson • all are in sequential order	• sentences address all major events in the lesson • all are in sequential order	• writing addresses all major events from the lesson • paragraph has clear topic sentence with adequate supporting details

© Harcourt

Build Background

Access Prior Knowledge

Tell students that they will talk about change. Make a four-column chart on chart paper. Head the columns: *People, Schools, Communities.* Leave the heading for the fourth column blank. Ask: *How do people change? How do schools change? How do communities change?* Record students' ideas in the appropriate columns.

• Before **Introduce**, p. 212
• 30 minutes

Lesson Vocabulary

Write *territory* on the board. Explain that a territory is land that belongs to a country but is not a state. Show a map. Point to and identify various states. Then point to Puerto Rico, and identify it as a United States territory. Write *pioneer.* Remind students of the words *settler* and *colonist.* Explain that a pioneer also goes to a new land to live. A pioneer goes to a place where no one or only a few people live. Write *immigrant.* Explain that an immigrant also moves to a new place. Immigrants move from one country to another. Write *civil war.* Explain that *civil* means something to do with people or citizens of a certain place. Ask: *Who might fight each other in a civil war?* Write *amend* on the board. Explain that it means "to change." Write *amendment.* Explain that an amendment is a change to something written. *I want to make an amendment to my letter. What else could we amend?*

Additional Vocabulary Explain that *made a home* may mean "to build a home." In this lesson, however, it means "to choose a place to live." *I made my home here.* Review other words or phrases in the margin in the context of the lesson, and have students make their own sentences.

face (v.)	made up of
hard	move
interpreter	stretched
journal	supply
made a home	view

Cognates As students read the lesson, you may wish to point out cognates such as: **territory/territorio, pioneer/pionero, immigrant/inmigrante.**

Build Fluency

Read aloud the following rhyme, and point out the words that sound alike. Return to the rhyme throughout the lesson to help develop vocabulary, sequence skills, and lesson content.

In the 1800s, our country began to expand.
We added the **territory** of Louisiana to our land.
Pioneers yelled, "West we go!"
And moved to a land they did not know.
The trip was hard and full of fears
As wagons rolled through new frontiers.
Later, trains chugged along a railroad track
Taking people from east to west and back.
Immigrants helped our country to grow.
They still do today, as you know.
We have settled our land in each and every place.
Now we are busy exploring the territory in space!

© Harcourt

Scaffolding the Content

Preview the Lesson

Explain to students that this lesson tells about ways the United States changed in the 1800s and 1900s. Revisit the chart for "Access Prior Knowledge." Write *United States* above the fourth column. Have students look at the headings and pictures to predict changes the lesson may tell about. Record ideas on the chart. At the end of the lesson, revisit the column, and have students check off the predictions that were correct.

• During **Teach**, pp. 212–219
• 30 minutes

Modify Instruction

Explain to students that there are reasons for things that happen. Tell them that as they read and talk about the lesson, they should think about the reasons things happened. Tell them that they will be adding reasons to a What and Why organizer.

1. **Exploring the Land** Explain that in 1803, President Thomas Jefferson bought a big piece of land for the United States. It was called the Louisiana Purchase. The president asked Meriwether Lewis and William Clark to explore the land. (Call attention to the area on the picture on page 213.) Other people helped them explore. Sacagawea was a Native American who helped to explore the land. Lewis and Clark learned many things about the West. Provide time for students to make a note on the What and Why organizer.

2. **Moving West** Point out that Lewis and Clark wrote about what they saw. Other people wanted to see the land, too. People started to move to the West. Some moved because they could not find jobs and land in the East. Explain that we call the people that moved pioneers. Their trip was hard. They rode in covered wagons. People got sick and hurt. They had bad weather. Sometimes, they fought with Native Americans on the way. Life was hard in the West. Pause for students to add ideas to the What and Why organizer.

3. **The Civil War** Tell students that people in the North thought that slavery was wrong. The people in the South wanted to have slaves work on their farms. A terrible war started in 1861. It was called the Civil War. The southern states said they did not want to be part of the United States any more. President Abraham Lincoln thought this was wrong. He thought slavery was wrong, too. He wrote a paper called the Emancipation Proclamation. It said that all enslaved people were free. In 1865, the war ended at last. Have students add to their organizers.

4. **Growing into Today's World** Point out that many other changes happened to the United States. In 1869, the first trains ran from the East to the West. Explain that this made it easier for people to travel to other communities. Also, ships brought people from other countries. Some wanted to stay and live here. We call them immigrants. We also added two new states, Alaska and Hawaii. Have students complete their organizers.

Extend

Have each student select one of the people mentioned in the lesson. Ask them to use simple biographies, the Internet, and other sources to gather facts about that person. Ask each student to make and present a poster about the individual.

• After **Teach**, pp. 212–219
• 30 minutes

What and Why

What happened?		Why?
Many people wanted to see the Louisiana Territory.	→	
More and more people settled in the West.	→	
The North and South fought the Civil War.	→	
More people started to travel.	→	
The United States grew.	→	

School-Home Connection Have students take this page home to share with their families. They can use the information on the organizer to tell about changes in the United States, and explain reasons for those changes.

© Harcourt

Apply and Assess

Write a Journal Entry

• During **Close**, p. 219
• 20 minutes

Make available picture books about pioneers who went to the West. Provide time for students to browse through the books with partners. Ask them to look for pictures that show how people traveled West and mark them with a sticky note. Then have pairs show their pictures to the class. Lead the class in discussing the pictures. Tell students to use the ideas they discussed to write their journal entries.

- Permit beginning students to create labeled picture entries.

- Have intermediate students write simple sentences in their journal entries. Invite them to include illustrations.

- Ask advanced students to tell about things they see, hear, smell, taste, and feel on their journey.

Informal Lesson Assessment

	Beginning	Intermediate	Advanced
Task	Students draw and label pictures of changes discussed in the lesson.	Students list phrases about changes in the United States during the 1800s and 1900s.	Provide an outline with the major subheadings of the lesson. Students fill out the outline with sentences about changes.
Below Expectations	• pictures are irrelevant • cannot verbalize ideas about the pictures	• listed items are irrelevant • list consists of words, not phrases • cannot verbally elaborate on the list	• sentences are irrelevant • responses are words or phrases, not sentences
Meets Expectations	• pictures show a few changes • uses words and phrases to verbalize ideas about the pictures	• lists a few changes • can elaborate verbally about the list	• provides at least one idea for each area of the outline • most responses are in sentence form
Above Expectations	• pictures show most of the changes discussed in the lesson • uses phrases to tell about the pictures	• lists most of the changes discussed in the lesson • uses oral sentences to elaborate on the list	• provides more than one sentence for each area of the outline • all responses are in sentence form

© Harcourt

Developing Academic Language

Throughout this unit, students will be asked to summarize social studies content in their own words. When summarizing, students should identify the main ideas or events in a passage. This strategy helps students internalize and remember the information they read.

Introduce Summarize

In brief sentences with a predictable pattern, summarize for students the events of the current day. For example: *Today was busy. We practiced fractions. We did a science experiment. We learned about the United States.* Write your sentences on the board, and have students read them with you. Point out that you did not tell everything that happened that day. Instead, you told about the most important parts of the day. Write the word *summarize* on the board. *Say: I told the main parts of the day. I summarized what happened today. When we summarize a book or paragraph, we use our own words to tell the most important parts.*

• Before **Summarize**, p. 236
• 25 minutes

Practice

To help students summarize, use an overhead projector to display a short story. Read the story to the class. Use a red marker to mark the key facts in the story. Then explain: *These are the important ideas of the story. We need to use our own words to make a short version, or summary, of the story.* Encourage students to suggest words or phrases to summarize the story's important points. Help them complete the following sentence frame: *This story is mostly about _____.*

Apply

Ask students to copy the chart below on a separate sheet of paper. Tell them that before they can summarize, they must read or listen to an entire passage. Then they must explain the passage in their own words. Together, look through a nonfiction book or news article. Help students identify an important fact. Then ask students to find another important fact. They should write the facts on the left side of the chart and then, in their own words, write a summary based on those facts. Gradually provide less help until students can work independently.

Key Fact	Summary
	This passage is mostly about
Key Fact	
Key Fact	

Build Background

Access Prior Knowledge

Invite students to tell or draw pictures about things they enjoy doing. Then have students complete this sentence: *I have the freedom to _____.* (sing, play, other activities students enjoy) Write the word *freedom* on the board, and say it with the group. Then write the word equation *freedom = rights,* and say the word *rights* with the group. Explain that rights are the freedoms we have in the United States.

• Before **Introduce**, p. 244
• 30 minutes

Lesson Vocabulary

Hold a mini-election with the group. Choose something simple to vote on, like a group name. Narrow the choices to two, then write both choices on slips of paper for each student. Tell students to draw a checkmark next to their choice. Collect the papers, and declare a winner. Then tell students that they have been part of an **election.** Point to the slips of paper, and say: ***Ballot.*** Encourage students to explain the purpose of a ballot, based on the activity. Then write ***majority rule*** on the board. Isolate *majority,* and say: *the most.* Say: *The* majority rule *is what the most people want.* Write ***minority rights*** on the board, isolate *minority,* and say: *the least.* Remind students of the word *rights* from "Access Prior Knowledge," and help them put the two terms together to form a definition: *The least amount of people—the* minority—*still have freedoms*—rights.

Additional Vocabulary Review other words or phrases in the margin in the context of the lesson, and have students make their own sentences.

Cognates As students read the lesson, you may wish to point out cognates such as: **constitution/constitución, election/elección, in public/en público, opinion/opinión.**

amendment	practice (religion)
assembly	press
Bill of Rights	respect
gather	rights
mistreat	rule

Build Fluency

Read aloud the following rhyme, and point out the words that sound alike. Return to the rhyme to help develop vocabulary, summarizing skills, and lesson content.

Rights are freedoms that we enjoy,
Every man and woman, girl and boy.
Some rights we get as we grow older,
Like voting in **elections** to choose our leaders.
We **elect** the people who will lead.
We mark our **ballot** for no one else to read.
The people who win have the **majority rule.**
But **minority rights** are protected, too.
Rights are the things that keep us free!
Every woman and man, you and me!

Scaffolding the Content

Preview the Lesson

• During **Teach**, pp. 244–247
• 30 minutes

Write the word *rights* on the board again, and check whether students can read and recognize it. Have students find the word in the lesson headings. Turn to page 245, and explore the photographs. Explain that each photograph shows the rights of citizens. Encourage students to describe what they see, and relate student comments to a particular right, or freedom:

- The girl is talking into the microphone = freedom of speech
- The people are in a church = freedom of religion
- The students are gathered together = freedom of assembly
- The girl is looking at a newspaper = freedom of the press

Explain that they will learn more about rights of citizens in this lesson.

Modify Instruction

Reproduce and pass out two copies of the blackline master. Have students find the words in the top box on the first page of the lesson, and agree that the words are *Rights of Citizens.* Below the heading, have them write the word equation *rights* = _____. Ask students if they recall another word for *rights,* and have students write *freedoms* to complete the word equation. Also review that a *citizen* is a person who lives in a place. Tell students that they will complete the blackline master as they explore the chapter.

1. **The Bill of Rights** Have students write *Bill of Rights* in the next box of the chart, and then have them skim the text on page 244 for the word *Constitution.* Point to the Constitution photograph and say: *The Constitution was written a long time ago. The Constitution tells about the rights of citizens.* Tell students to write *Constitution* in the Bill of Rights box. Turn to page 245, and have students read the captions on the photographs. Ask students what all these freedoms have in common, and agree that these freedoms are rights of citizens. Let students act out these freedoms as they write each in a circle on their graphic organizers.

2. **Citizens Make Choices** Pass out the second graphic organizer, read the top box with students, and then have students write *Citizens Make Choices* in the second box. Also have students write the word equation *citizens = people* below it. Tell students to write the word *election* in one circle, and *ballot* in another. Have them recall the meaning of these words and then draw pictures in the circles to show their meanings. In the last two circles, have them write *majority rule* and *minority rights.* Encourage students to remember which term means *the most* and which means *the least,* and have them write *most* and *least* in the correct circles. Return to the chant to review these terms.

Extend

• After **Teach**, pp. 244–247
• 10 minutes

Have students consider which of the four rights in this lesson they use the most in their life. Have students write "Freedom of _____" at the top of a sheet of paper and then illustrate themselves enjoying that right.

© Harcourt

Name _____ Date _____

DIRECTIONS Complete this chart to show what our rights are.

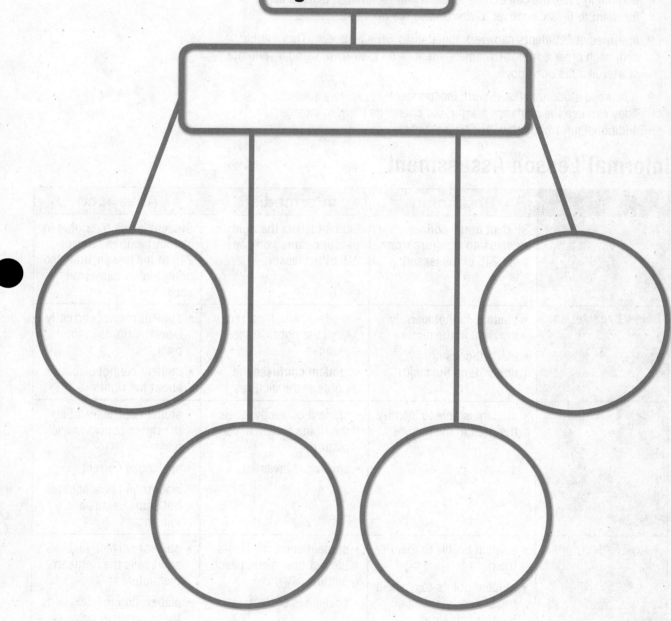

What Are Our Rights?

Rights of Citizens

 School-Home Connection Have students take their graphic organizers home to show their families. Ask them to explain the difference between the various meanings of *rights, right,* and *write.* Then have them act out for their families the rights that citizens enjoy.

Unit 4, Chapter 7, Lesson 1

Success for English Learners ▪ 95

© Harcourt

Apply and Assess

Write a Speech

• During **Close**, p. 247
• 30 minutes

Write the word *speech* on the board, and ask students which picture in the lesson shows someone *giving a speech*. Agree that it is the girl at the top left of page 245. Suggest that her speech tells about the rights of citizens in the United States. What might she say? Work with students to write such a speech.

- Beginning students can dictate ideas to you. You might begin a sentence for them to finish, such as: *Citizens have the right to* _____.

- Intermediate students can work together to write a speech. They should help each other compose simple sentences on their own, using a sentence starter like the one above.

- Advanced students should work independently to write a speech. They can use the sentence starter, but challenge them to include additional information about citizens' rights.

Informal Lesson Assessment

	Beginning	**Intermediate**	**Advanced**
Task	Student orally defines a *right*, using a picture from page 245 of the lesson.	Student labels the rights in all four pictures on page 245 of the lesson.	Student labels the rights in all four pictures on page 245 of the lesson, and also orally elaborates about each.
Below Expectations	• student cannot identify the right in the picture • student does not understand the task	• student cannot correctly label the rights in the pictures • student confuses the rights in the pictures	• student cannot correctly label the rights in the pictures • student cannot elaborate about the rights
Meets Expectations	• student is able to identify the right in the picture	• student correctly labels the rights shown in each picture • spelling is invented	• student correctly labels the rights shown in each picture • spelling is correct • elaboration is adequate, but some details are missing
Above Expectations	• student is able to identify the right • student points to clues in the picture that helped identify this right	• student correctly labels the rights shown in each picture • spelling is correct	• student correctly labels and spells the rights in the pictures • elaboration fully explains these rights of citizens

© Harcourt

Build Background

Access Prior Knowledge

Have students list classroom responsibilities, such as throwing trash away, pushing chairs under desks, and so on. Say this sentence starter for students to complete for each responsibility: *We have to _____.* Let students offer their own ideas for things they must do in class. Say: *These things make us good citizens at school.*

• Before **Introduce**, p. 248
• 20 minutes

Lesson Vocabulary

Write the word **responsibility** on the board. Say: *Things we have to do are* responsibilities. *Responsibilities make us good citizens.* Then ask students what might happen if they did not perform one of these tasks, such as if they did not throw away trash. Write the word **consequence** on the board. Say: *When we do not do our responsibilities, there is a* consequence. Write the phrase **common good** on the board. Have students explain what *good* means. Then, explain that the *common good* means things that are good for everyone. Next, tell students you need a **volunteer** to help hold up word cards. After a volunteer has been chosen, encourage students to explain the word on their own. For the word **jury**, have students turn to page 249 of the lesson and point to the people sitting in the box. Explain that these people make a jury. They have a responsibility. Finally, have the volunteer holding the word cards present each vocabulary word. Encourage students to read each card.

Additional Vocabulary Review the words or phrases in the margin in the context of the lesson, and have students make their own sentences. For example, hold up a craft stick, and ask a student to break it. Review the meaning of *law,* and then ask students how someone might *break a law.* Help them realize that breaking a law means not following it.

Cognates As students read the lesson, you may wish to point out cognates such as: **consequence/consecuencia, respect/respetar, responsibility/responsabilidad.**

breaks the law
face (consequences)
(pay a) fine
limit
peacefully
raise money
right
settle
taxes

Build Fluency

Read aloud the following rhyme, and point out the words that sound alike. Return to the rhyme to help develop vocabulary, summarizing skills, and lesson content.

Citizens have **responsibilities,** or duties, they must do. These duties help the **common good.** Here are a few: Citizens must follow laws, and pay their taxes, too. They also must be on a **jury.** It's the thing to do. Citizens can **volunteer** to help people in need. Citizens have responsibilities. They do, indeed. **Consequences** happen when duties aren't done. If you do your responsibility, you'll be helping everyone!

© Harcourt

Scaffolding the Content

Preview the Lesson

Review with students the responsibilities they have in class. Remind them that these responsibilities make them good citizens in school. Turn to the lesson, and have students find the word *responsibilities* on page 248, as well as the word *citizens*. Ask students whether they think that citizens of a community have responsibilities. Brainstorm with students responsibilities that citizens might have. Let students act out their suggested responsibilities, as needed, and list ideas on the board. Tell students to look for any of these ideas as they explore the lesson.

• During **Teach**, pp. 248–251
• 25 minutes

Modify Instruction

Read the lesson title for students, and ask them to say another word that means the same as *duties*. Agree that it is *responsibilities,* and ask students to find *responsibility* in the first paragraph. Then pass out the graphic organizer to each student, and review the page title and the words *duty* and *responsibilities*. Have students complete the blackline master to tell about the duties of citizens.

1. **Our Responsibilities** Share with students key words from this section: *obey laws, pay taxes, serve on a jury.* Tell students to write each on a line on their graphic organizers under "Our Responsibilities." Then have students draw simple pictures or symbols that illustrate each. For example, for *obey laws*, students could draw a stop sign. For *pay taxes*, students could draw bills and coins. You might explain that taxes are money that people pay to the government. For *serve on a jury*, students could draw a person sitting in a box, like the people on page 249. Explain that a jury meets in a place called a courtroom. Arrange students' chairs to resemble a jury box to reinforce the word. Ask students what these three things have in common, and agree that we must do these things because it is the law. Have students write *It is the law* outside the box.

2. **Serving Your Community** Ask students whether we have responsibilities that are not because of the law. Have students write *It is not the law* outside the second box. Then call out these key phrases from this section: *work for the common good* and *volunteer.* Have students write them on the lines under "Serving Your Community." Encourage students to recall the meaning of *common good* and *volunteer.* Have students draw pictures to show something citizens can do for the common good, such as throwing away trash. Have students describe what they see in the pictures on pages 250 and 251. Explain that these people have *volunteered* to help someone. Have students draw pictures to show someone volunteering to help others.

Extend

Ask students to think about their own community. Have each student draw a picture of him or herself being responsible in the community. For example, the student might wait for a light to turn green before crossing a street, walk a dog on a leash, or help a neighbor. Encourage students to share their pictures, and tell about the responsibility they have illustrated.

• After **Teach**, pp. 248–251
• 15 minutes

Name _____ Date _____

Duties of Citizens

Our Responsibilities

1. _____

2. _____

3. _____

●

Serving Your Community

1. _____

2. _____

● **School-Home Connection** Ask students to take their graphic organizers home to share with their families. Tell students to ask their families which responsibilities their families have done. Encourage students to add to their charts any ideas their families have about the duties of citizens.

Apply and Assess

Write a Report

• During **Close**, p. 251
• 30 minutes

Make sure students understand that a report is something that is written; a report tells information. You might show to the group sample reports that students have written. Then ask students to write a report about what people can do to be responsible citizens.

- Beginning students can draw a picture of a citizen acting responsibly, and dictate a caption that you write.

- Intermediate students can be jump-started with a sentence starter, such as: *Responsible citizens should _____.* They can then work with partners to complete it.

- Advanced students should be challenged to write a report on their own about being a responsible citizen. Allow them to use the headings and information in the lesson to prompt their writing.

Informal Lesson Assessment

	Beginning	Intermediate	Advanced
Task	Student says a key word or phrase, describing one responsibility as a citizen, and then acts it out.	Student uses phrases or short sentences to tell about one responsibility of citizens and acts it out.	Student uses complete sentences to tell about one or more responsibilities of citizens while acting them out.
Below Expectations	• student cannot express idea verbally • student cannot express idea through pantomime	• student cannot express ideas in a complete sentence • student's actions do not reflect ideas	• student names none or only one responsibility • student's actions do not reflect ideas
Meets Expectations	• student expresses idea with a key word • student expresses idea through pantomime	• student expresses idea in a complete sentence • student's actions match ideas expressed in the sentence	• student correctly identifies two or more responsibilities • actions reflect ideas • words are slightly mispronounced or sentences are poorly constructed
Above Expectations	• student expresses idea in a complete sentence	• student suggests more than one responsibility • student elaborates	• student correctly identifies and acts out several responsibilities • words and sentences are spoken with very little error

Chapter 7

Build Background

Access Prior Knowledge

Ask students to name things (or qualities) they like about their friends, and list ideas on the board. For example, students might express that a friend is caring, helpful, loyal, or fun to be with. Review students' ideas, asking students to complete a sentence, such as: *A good friend is _____.* Then ask students if these same qualities could tell about citizens. Have students complete this sentence with the same ideas: *A good citizen is _____.*

• Before **Introduce**, p. 252
• 20 minutes

Lesson Vocabulary

Circle all the ideas students suggested for the qualities of a good friend, and above the circle, write the term *character trait.* Say the phrase, then point to the words within the circle, and say: *These are good qualities. These are good character traits.* Help students connect character traits to the qualities people have. Write *cooperate* on the board, and have students say it with you. Have pairs of students work together to spell and write the word, and then explain that working together is cooperating. Write the remaining vocabulary words on the board: **justice, boycott, hero.** Say them for the group. Provide explanations for each word, and challenge students to match the definition with each word. For further reinforcement, invite students to use the words in sentences.

Additional Vocabulary Review words or phrases in the margin in the context of the lesson, and have students make their own sentences.

Cognates As students read the lesson, you may wish to point out cognates such as: **action/acción, boycott/boicot, character/carácter, cooperate/cooperar, justice/justicia.**

boycott	show respect
bring change	speak out
follow (the law)	take action
quality (n.)	take part in
sets an example	unfair

Build Fluency

Read aloud the following rhyme, and point out the words that sound alike. Return to the rhyme to help develop vocabulary, summarizing skills, and lesson content.

Being a good citizen is not that hard to do.
Good citizens have qualities. We can list a few.
Good citizens **cooperate.** They work well with each other.
Good citizens are caring, too, and helping is no bother.
Good citizens speak out for fairness. They may work a lot.
They may refuse to do or buy things. This is a **boycott.**
Good citizens are sometimes **heroes,** always brave and strong.
Good citizens have **character traits** that help them get along.

© Harcourt

Scaffolding the Content

Preview the Lesson

Ask students to scan the lesson, paying attention to the headings. Ask students what they notice about the headings. Point out that most of the headings are people's names: Jimmy Carter, Rosa Parks, and Dolores Huerta.

Read these names with the group, and write them on the board. Then ask students why these people are in a chapter about being a good citizen. Agree that as students explore the chapter, they will learn more about the qualities that make these three people good citizens. Let students tell what they know about these three people, if anything.

- During **Teach**, pp. 252–257
- 30 minutes

Modify Instruction

Give each student a copy of the blackline master. Say the name of each person, and have students recognize and point to that name on their papers. Then invite students to complete their charts as they explore this chapter about being good citizens.

1 **What Is a Good Citizen?** Have students find this title on their charts, and then have them share their own ideas about good citizens. Write ideas on the board, and have students try to find examples in the text, such as: *follow laws, speak out against things that are unfair, doing their best, being responsible, having respect,* and *helping others.* Tell students to write these ideas in the top box of their blackline masters.

2 **Jimmy Carter** Have students draw a picture of Jimmy Carter under his name in the first column of the chart. Have students listen closely as you read the text. Then point to the picture on page 254, and say: *These people are building houses. Jimmy Carter helps build homes for people. He is a good citizen.* Ask students to write or draw this idea on their charts.

3 **Rosa Parks** Continue in this way with Rosa Parks. First, have students draw her picture in the first column. Then point to the picture on page 255, and say: *Rosa Parks helped change laws. She made laws fair so that everyone could ride the buses. She was a good citizen.* Have students write and draw these ideas on their charts.

4 **Dolores Huerta** Continue in this manner with Dolores Huerta. Point to the picture on page 256, and say: *Dolores Huerta wanted to help farm workers. She helped make life better for farmworkers. She was a good citizen.* Have students note these ideas on the chart.

5 **Everyday Heroes** Ask students what *everyday* might mean. Explain that you do not have to be famous to be a good citizen; we see good citizens every day! Have students write *firefighters, police officers, teachers,* and *volunteers* in the last part of the chart, and then write qualities that make them everyday heroes.

Extend

Ask students to think about an everyday hero in the community. Have students draw a picture of this person, and write his or her name. Work with students to write a sentence or two about the hero. Then combine students' pages into an "Everyday Heroes" book.

- After **Teach**, pp. 252–257
- 15 minutes

© Harcourt

DIRECTIONS Complete this chart to tell about good citizens and the qualities they have.

Being a Good Citizen

What Is a Good Citizen?

Who Are Good Citizens?	Why Are They Good Citizens? What Qualities Do They Have?
Jimmy Carter	
Rosa Parks	
Dolores Huerta	
Everyday Heroes	

School-Home Connection Tell students to take their charts home to show their families. Tell students to discuss someone they know who they think is a good citizen. Have them identify the qualities this person has. Ask students to write about this person on the back of their graphic organizers.

Apply and Assess

Make a Poster

Point to posters you have hanging around the room, or unroll a poster to share with students. Ask students to point out what is special about a poster, such as its large heading, colorful pictures, or short sections of information. Then tell students that you would like them to make posters to tell about two qualities good citizens have: justice and respect.

• During **Close**, p. 257
• 30 minutes

- Beginning students should write *justice and respect* in big letters on their poster papers, and then dictate sentences to you about the words.

- Intermediate students should write the heading *justice and respect* on their poster paper, and then work with partners to discuss the meanings of these words and how they can illustrate them.

- Advanced students should work independently, incorporating *justice and respect* into their posters, along with short paragraphs and illustrations that reflect their ideas.

Informal Lesson Assessment

	Beginning	Intermediate	Advanced
Task	Student completes the sentence *A good citizen is ____* with an appropriate quality or character trait.	Student completes the sentence *A good citizen is ____* with an appropriate quality or character trait, as well as an example.	Student explains two or more qualities of good citizens using his or her own words.
Below Expectations	• student does not understand the sentence • student cannot complete the sentence	• student does not understand the sentence • student cannot complete the sentence • student cannot provide an example	• student names no or only one quality • student's oral sentences are stilted with many errors
Meets Expectations	• student understands the sentence • student completes the sentence with an appropriate word or phrase	• student understands the sentence • student completes the sentence with an appropriate term • student provides an appropriate example	• student adequately explains two or more qualities • words are slightly mispronounced or sentences slightly misconstructed • some phrasing is borrowed from text
Above Expectations	• student provides an example or elaborates on ideas	• student suggests additional qualities of good citizens	• student's ideas are clearly expressed, using original sentences

© Harcourt

Chapter 8

Build Background

Access Prior Knowledge

Write the word *government* on the board, and say it aloud several times with the group. Ask students what they know about government. To prompt ideas, show them a picture of the president or point out a government symbol, like the flag or the Capitol. Elicit from students key concept words that might be familiar, like *leaders, laws, voting,* and *elections.*

• Before **Introduce**, p. 266
• 20 minutes

Lesson Vocabulary

Point to the word *government* again, and say it once more with the group. Write the word *service* after the word *government,* and say the entire phrase for students **(government service).** Lead students to figure out the meaning of *service* by saying: *Teachers teach. They provide a service. Police officers protect. They provide a service.* Ask students what they think *government service* means. Agree that a service is something a person does to help other people; a government service is something the government does to help people. Then say: *The government has **authority.*** Write *authority* on the board, and ask students what it might mean. Agree that authority means the right to tell others what to do. Finally, write *legislative, executive,* and *judicial* on the board. Point to the pictures of each branch of government on page 268. Read the question below the pictures to the class. Then ask similar questions, such as *Who writes the laws? Who makes sure laws are fair?*

Additional Vocabulary Review the words in the margin in the context of the lesson, and have students make their own sentences.

Cognates As students read the lesson, you may wish to point out cognates such as: **authority/autoridad, conflict/conflicto, executive/ejecutivo/-a, judicial/judicial, legislative/legislativo/-a, local/local, national/nacional.**

branch	national
federal	state
level	structure
local	

Build Fluency

Read aloud the following rhyme, and point out the words that sound alike. Return to the chant throughout the lesson to help develop vocabulary, summarizing skills, and reinforce lesson content.

Understanding our government is not hard.
Remember that it has three levels, or parts.
Local government has **authority** only in the town.
The state government can use its power all around.
The national government works for all the United States.
Here you'll find three branches that cooperate—
Legislative, judicial, and **executive,** too.
Government services help me and you.
Understanding our government is not hard to do!

Scaffolding the Content

Preview the Lesson

• During **Teach**, pp. 266–269
• 20 minutes

To help students make the connection between levels and branches of government, draw another tree on the board. Tell students to think of this tree as a tree that tells them about the government.

- The bottom of the tree is for small communities, like towns. Label this portion of your tree *towns.*

- The middle of the tree is for state communities. Label this portion of your tree *states.*

- The leafy, full part of the tree is for the government that rules over the entire United States. Label this portion of the tree *nation.*

Motion to these three levels—towns, states, nation—and explain that students will learn about the government for each. Ask students to guess why the United States needs three levels of government.

Modify Instruction

Pass out copies of the blackline master to each student. Have them match the trees on their charts with the tree you drew on the board. Encourage students to write the words *towns, states,* and *nation* on their activity sheets. Then begin to explore the lesson.

1. **The Levels of Government** Help students recall the meaning of level by asking them to move their hands up and down to show a high, or top, level and a low, or bottom, level. Have them point to top, middle, and bottom levels on their trees as you say *nation, states, towns.* Have students find the word *town* at the top of page 267 and the word that tells about its government *(local).* Tell them to write *local* on the tree trunk. Have them find the word *states* and the word that tells about this type of government *(state).* Have them write *state* on the tree trunk. Then have them find the word *nation* and the type of government that the nation, or country, has *(federal or national).* Tell them to write *federal* in the boughs of the tree, as well as the word *national,* another word for federal. Name a local, state, or national government official that all the students would know. Ask students which level of government the person is from.

2. **The Branches of Government** Ask students to say *federal government, national government,* then ask them to finger-trace the branches in the tree's bough. Explain that the government of the nation, or the United States, has three branches. Challenge students to recall the words they learned during Lesson Vocabulary: executive, judicial, legislative. Have students write each word in a branch. Then say a word that tells what each branch does, and have students figure out the branch, using a "letter riddle." For example, exaggerate the *l* in *law,* and ask students which branch makes laws *(legislative).* Exaggerate the *j* in *judge,* and ask which branch has judges that make sure the laws are fair *(judicial).* Which branch is left? Which branch is the president a part of? *(executive)*

Extend

• After **Teach**, pp. 266–269
• 5 minutes

Help students identify their local and state governments. For example, what is the name of their town? Their town has its own government. What is the name of their state? Their state has its own government. Finally, what is the name of their nation?

© Harcourt

Name _____ Date _____

● **DIRECTIONS** Complete this tree to tell about the structure of government.

The Structure of Government

The Branches of Government

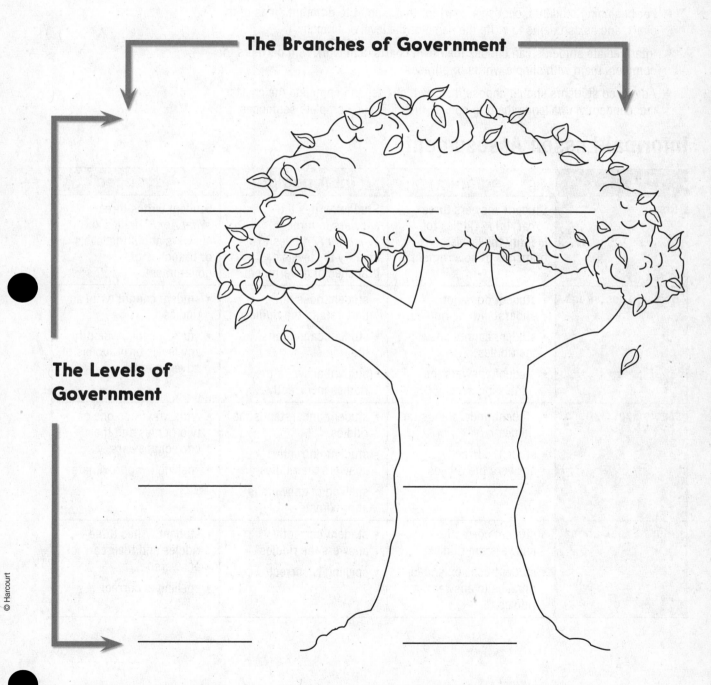

●

The Levels of Government

_____

_____

● **School-Home Connection** Have students take their government trees home to share with their families. Encourage students to identify the levels and branches of government and to identify for their families the name of their town, state, and nation.

© Harcourt

Apply and Assess

Make a Chart

Draw different types of charts on the board, such as a chart with columns and a flow chart. Ask students to choose a format they think would work best to tell about the levels and branches of government. Encourage students to use the information on their "Structure of Government" trees as they work.

• During **Close**, p. 269
• 30 minutes

- For beginning students, choose a chart for them, point to different areas of the chart, and ask students to write the name of the level or branch.

- Intermediate students can choose their own charts, and work with partners to complete them with simple words or phrases.

- Advanced students should choose their own charts, and complete the charts independently. Challenge them to convey their ideas in complete sentences.

Informal Lesson Assessment

	Beginning	Intermediate	Advanced
Task	Student answers three *What Am I?* riddles to identify the levels or branches of government.	Student writes the answers to three *What Am I?* riddles to identify the levels or branches of government.	Student writes three *What Am I?* riddles and answers about the levels or branches of government.
Below Expectations	• student does not understand the riddles • student cannot answer the riddles • student answers the riddles incorrectly	• student does not understand the riddles • student cannot answer the riddles • student answers the riddles incorrectly	• student cannot write any riddles • student cannot identify any levels or branches of government
Meets Expectations	• student understands the riddles • student correctly answers the riddles	• student understands the riddles • student correctly answers the riddles • spelling of answers is approximate	• student writes one or two riddles and their correct answers • spelling is approximate
Above Expectations	• student correctly answers the riddles • student uses extended phrases to answer the riddles	• student correctly answers the riddles • spelling is correct	• student writes three riddles and their correct answers • spelling is correct

© Harcourt

Build Background

Access Prior Knowledge

Have students recall the levels of government, starting with the top level, or federal government. Name the United States president, and ask students which level of government he works for. Then name your state, and ask students what this type of government is called (state government). Then name your town, and ask students what type of government it has (local government). Have students share what they know about local government.

• Before **Introduce**, p. 272
• 20 minutes

Lesson Vocabulary

Write *county, council, court,* and *county seat* on the board, and help students distinguish them. For example, have a volunteer point out that *court* has the letter *r* and *county* ends with the letter *y*. Use the word cards as well, and challenge students to distinguish the words as you hold up each card. Then introduce students to the remaining vocabulary words: **mayor, recreation, public works.** Ask students which word tells about someone who leads a community (mayor); which tells about fun activities (recreation); and which tells about services for everyone (public works).

Additional Vocabulary Write these multiple-meaning words on the board: *run, board, works, plant.* Have students gesture to show their understanding of each (students might run in place for *run,* point to a classroom plant for *plant,* point to a flat surface for *board,* or pantomime doing homework for *work*). Help students locate each word in the text (*run,* page 273; *board,* page 274; *works* and *plants,* page 277), and use context to figure out the meanings in the lesson.

board
plant
run
works

Cognates As students read the lesson, you may wish to point out cognates such as: **department/departamento, education/educación, police/policía, recreation/recreación.**

Build Fluency

Read aloud the following rhyme, and point out the words that sound alike. Return to the chant throughout the lesson to help develop vocabulary, summarizing skills, and reinforce lesson content. This chant can be loosely sung to "Here We Go 'Round the Mulberry Bush."

The **mayor** is the local leader,
Local leader, local leader,
The mayor is the local leader,
In charge of the local **council.**
The government works at the **county seat,**
This is where leaders meet.
The government works at the county seat,
This is the **county** government.
Courts and **recreation,** too,
Public works, for me and you.
Courts and recreation, too—
Are run by your local government.

© Harcourt

Scaffolding the Content

Preview the Lesson

Turn to the beginning of the lesson, and ask students to predict what the lesson will be about. Agree that it will tell about local governments. Have students read these words in the lesson title. Then ask students to predict which three aspects of local government they will learn about, and have them refer to the main headings.

• During **Teach**, pp. 272–277
• 20 minutes

Modify Instruction

Introduce students to the blackline master on the next page. Pass out copies of the chart, and have students identify its shape (triangle). Have students read the title at the top of the triangle, and suggest that students match it with the lesson title: Local Governments. Have students find the three main lesson headings: *City and Town Government; County Government; Community Services.* Have students write each heading in the second level of the triangle, below Local Government. Explain that as they explore the lesson, they will learn about these areas of local government.

1. **City and Town Government** Point out the words *council* and *mayor* on page 273. Tell students to write them on the bottom level of their triangles, below "City and Town Government." To explain a council, use your arm to indicate a small group of students, and have them talk about a local problem, such as dirty streets. Tell the class that the group is the council. A council is a group of people who make decisions for the city government. Then choose one student, and say: *You are the mayor. The mayor is the leader.* Write *legislative branch* and *executive branch* on the board. Ask students which branches a city council and mayor belong to (city council belongs to the legislative branch; the mayor belongs to the executive branch).

2. **County Government** If your community is part of a county, name the county. Point to the map of New Jersey on page 274, and ask students what the lines dividing the state mean. Agree that these show smaller parts of the state, called counties. Have students write *county board, county seat,* and *county courts* on the bottom level of their triangles below "County Government." Have students look through the text for key words that tell about each, such as *laws, offices,* and *judges.* Ask students if a county board is part of the executive or legislative branch of government (legislative).

3. **Community Services** Have students turn to page 276, and identify what they see in the photographs. Ask students what else might be a community service. Have students look in the text for ideas, such as: *police, school, sports, parks.* Ask students to find *trash* under *public works,* then to explain what public works might refer to. Tell students to write key words about community services on the bottom row of their triangles.

Extend

Give each student four sheets of paper. On one sheet, have them create a book cover with the title "Local Governments." On the remaining three sheets, ask them to draw pictures that show three or more things their local government does for them. Encourage students to write text for their pictures. Staple the pages together to form books.

• After **Teach**, pp. 272–277
• 20 minutes

© Harcourt

Name _____ Date _____

Fill out this triangle to tell about local governments.

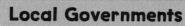

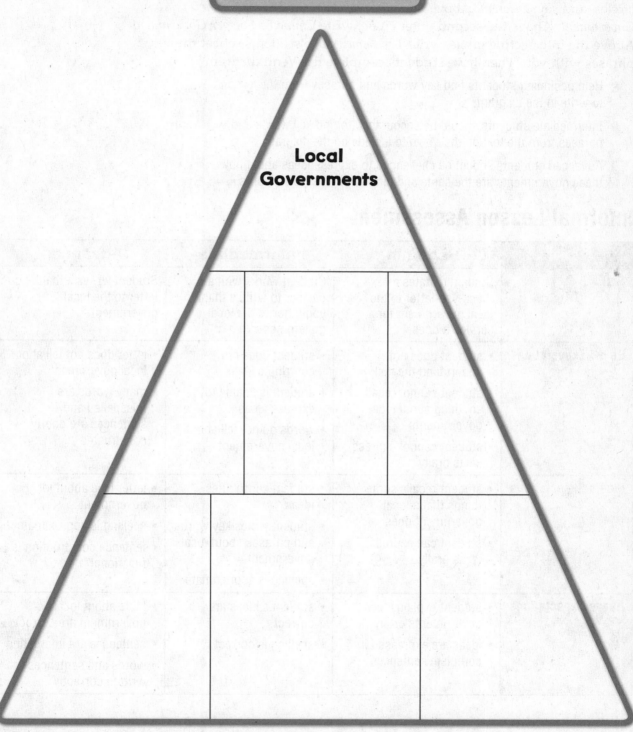

Local Governments

 School-Home Connection Have students take their "Local Government" triangles home to share with their families. Students can first ask their families what they know about local governments, and then explain about local governments, using the information on their triangles.

© Harcourt

Apply and Assess

Make a Diagram

• During **Close**, p. 277
• 45 minutes

Draw a Venn diagram on the board, and review its function with the group. Point to the middle circle, and say: *the same*. Point to the outer circles, and say: *different*. Above one outer circle write *Mayor-Council Government*. Above the second outer circle, write *Council-Manager Government*. Above the intersecting circle, write *The Same*. Have students repeat these phrases with you. Then have students complete the Venn diagram.

- Help beginning students find key words and phrases from the lesson to write in the diagram.

- Intermediate students should be encouraged to find key words and phrases from the text on their own to include on the diagram.

- Advanced students should be challenged to express ideas about how these governments are the same and different in their own words.

Informal Lesson Assessment

	Beginning	Intermediate	Advanced
Task	Student dictates a thank-you letter to the local government for a service it does.	Student works with a partner to write a thank-you letter to the local government.	Student writes a thank-you letter to the local government.
Below Expectations	• student does not understand the task • student cannot recall anything about local governments • student cannot express ideas orally	• student does not contribute ideas • student is unable to express ideas • words do not tell about local government	• letter does not tell about local government • many words are misspelled and sentences are poorly constructed
Meets Expectations	• student recalls some things that a local government does • student can express ideas orally	• student contributes ideas • student writes key words and phrases about local government • spelling is approximate	• letter tells about local government • spelling is approximate • sentence construction is functional
Above Expectations	• student explains local governments orally • ideas are expressed in complete sentences	• student's ideas are correct • spelling is correct	• facts about local government are correct • sentences are interesting • words and sentences are written correctly

© Harcourt

Build Background

Access Prior Knowledge

Write *national government, state government,* and *local government* on the board, and say them with the group. Ask students which government tells about their community (local). Then ask which government tells about the United States (national). Say: *mayor, governor, president,* and write the words on the board. Have students match each leader with the type of government.

• Before **Introduce**, p. 280
• 20 minutes

Lesson Vocabulary

Use the photographs in the lesson to introduce the vocabulary words. Hold up the word cards for **capitol, Congress, representative,** and **supreme court.** One at a time, have students say the word, and then find the photo in the lesson (pages 281, 283, and 284). Finally, hold up the card for **appointed.** Point to one student in the group and say: *I appoint you to help me. I choose you to help me.* Repeat with other students, until they understand the meaning of **appoint.** Try to make clear the distinction between *elect* and *appoint.*

Additional Vocabulary Review words or phrases in the margin in the context of the lesson, and have students make their own sentences.

Cognates As students read the lesson, you may wish to point out cognates such as: **capital/capital, capitol/capitolio, governor/gobernador/-ora, postal/postal.**

capital
carried out
goods
retire

Build Fluency

Read aloud the following rhyme, and point out the words that sound alike. Return to the chant throughout the lesson to help develop vocabulary, summarizing skills, and reinforce lesson content. This chant can loosely be sung to "Are You Sleeping?"

State and national, state and national, governments!
Governments!
How are they the same? How are they different?
Let's find out. Let's find out.

State and national, state and national, governments!
Governments!
Both have these three branches—judicial and executive,
Legislative, too! Legislative, too!

National government, has a leader—the President!
The President!
It also has a **Congress,** with lots of **representatives,**
The **Supreme Court,** too. The Supreme Court, too.

State government, has a leader—**the governor!**
The governor!
It also has three branches—judicial, and executive,
Legislative too! Legislative too!

Scaffolding the Content

Preview the Lesson

• During **Teach**, pp. 280–285
• 20 minutes

This lesson explores how state governments and the national government are alike and different. To preview, show students a map of the United States, as well as a map of your state. Point to each map, and have students say the place that the map shows. Tell students that you will say words about government, and they should point to the map that tells whether the word is for the state or the United States government.

- Begin with *president* and *governor*.

- If available, show students a picture of your state capitol building, as well as the United States Capitol building.

- Then say: *executive branch*, *judicial branch*, *legislative branch*, and *supreme court*. Allow students to point to both maps, and explain these are some things that the national and state governments have in common. Tell students that they will learn more about these similarities and differences in the lesson.

Modify Instruction

Pass out copies of the blackline master page, and read the headings with the group. Make sure students realize that the first column lists things about government in general, the second column is for state governments, and the last column is for the national, or United States, government. Begin exploring state governments.

1 State Governments Have students look for the word *executive* in the first paragraph, and ask who works for the executive branch of the state government. Agree that it is the governor, and ask students to write *governor* in that box of their charts. Continue to page 281. Ask students to find *legislative* and *judicial*, and choose which other words to write in their charts that best tell about each. Students may also draw their ideas.

2 National Governments Move on to page 282. Have students find the word *executive* and the person who works for this government branch (the President). Continue on with *legislative* on page 283 and *judicial* on page 284, guiding students as needed to locate key words and phrases that tell about each branch. Also allow students to add illustrations. Help the group compare the information they have written for both state and national governments. Ask: *How are the governments the same? How are they different?*

3 State and National Services Finally, address the services provided by each form of government. Have students write key words and phrases in the appropriate column of the chart to tell about the services, such as *state parks*, *highways*, *goods* under "State Governments" and *mail*, *national parks*, *goods* under "National Government."

Extend

• After **Teach**, pp. 280–285
• 20 minutes

Divide the class in half. Tell one group that it is a state government and the other group that it is the national government. Have students work together within their groups to write simple sentences that tell about their government. Encourage students to use the ideas they wrote on their charts. Invite each group to share their work.

© Harcourt

Name _____ Date _____

State and National Governments

Things About the Government	The State Governments	The National Government
Executive Branch		
Legislative Branch		
Judicial Branch		
Services		

 School-Home Connection Have students take their charts home to show their families. Tell them to explain the purpose of the chart, and then to describe how the government of their state is the same and different from the national government.

© Harcourt

Apply and Assess

Write a Letter

• During **Close**, p. 285
• 40 minutes

Write *representative* on the board, and have students find a picture of a representative in the lesson. Ask students whether a representative could help them, and agree that a representative listens to problems. Hold up a letter that someone has written, and explain that people write letters to their government representatives to tell their problems. Then work with students to write their own letters to a state government representative.

- Talk with beginning students about a problem in the community. Have students draw a picture of the problem, and help them write a caption for it.

- Have intermediate students discuss ideas with a partner, and write simple sentences in a letter format.

- Encourage advanced students to develop ideas on their own, and to write complete and interesting sentences for their letters.

Informal Lesson Assessment

	Beginning	Intermediate	Advanced
Task	Student dictates ideas to help you complete a Venn diagram about national and state governments.	Student completes a Venn diagram with key words and phrases about national and state governments.	Student completes a Venn diagram with complete sentences about national and state governments.
Below Expectations	• student cannot tell how the governments are alike • student cannot tell how the governments are different • student does not understand the task	• words and/or phrases do not tell about the governments • diagram is only partially complete	• sentences do not tell about the governments • many words are misspelled and sentences are poorly constructed • diagram is only partially complete
Meets Expectations	• student is able to indicate similarities and differences, either orally or by pointing to pictures in the text	• words and/or phrases tell about the governments • diagram is complete • spelling is approximate	• sentences tell about the governments • spelling is approximate • diagram is complete
Above Expectations	• student orally describes similarities and differences in clear, complete sentences	• words and/or phrases tell about the governments • diagram is complete • spelling is correct	• sentences tell about the governments • sentences are correct and interesting • spelling is correct

© Harcourt

Build Background

Access Prior Knowledge

Write the word *symbol* on the board, and say it with the group. Review simple symbols with students. For example, draw the division symbol on the board, and ask students to explain or show what it means. Other symbols might include a dollar sign, a smiley face, a gold star, and so on. Then point to a patriotic symbol you have in class, such as the flag. Ask students what this symbol stands for, and agree that it is a symbol of the United States.

• Before **Introduce**, p. 290
• 20 minutes

Lesson Vocabulary

Write the word *patriotic* before the word *symbol* on the board. Say: *Patriotic means to feel good about one's country.* Point to the flag again, and say: *The flag is a **patriotic symbol**. A patriotic symbol is a good symbol about the country.* You might have students share patriotic symbols they recall from their own countries. Then hum a few bars of "The Star-Spangled Banner." Write the word **anthem** on the board, hum the anthem, and then say the word. Say: *An anthem is a song. An anthem is a song for a country.* Have students turn to page 292, and ask them to find the tall object in the picture. Have students trace the Washington Monument as they say the word **monument**. Write the word on the board. Say: Monuments *honor people or things that happened in the past.* Write the word **memorial** on the board, and have students find the word in the labels on page 292. Ask students for some ideas about why people build monuments.

Additional Vocabulary Review words or phrases in the margin in the context of the lesson, and have students make their own sentences.

Cognates As students read the lesson, you may wish to point out cognates such as: **attention/atención, column/columna, liberty/libertad, monument/monumento, patriotic/patriótico, patriotism/patriotismo, poem/poema, symbol/símbolo.**

feelings	marker
fort	stand at attention
lasting	

Build Fluency

Read aloud the following rhyme, and point out the words that sound alike. Return to the chant throughout the lesson to help develop vocabulary, summarizing skills, and reinforce lesson content.

A symbol stands for an idea, a simple way to show it.
A symbol stands for an idea; it is a way to know it.
Our country has some symbols that represent our nation.
Patriotic symbols show our love and dedication.
Wave the flag! Fly it high! It's a national symbol.
Sing the **anthem** loud with pride. It's a national symbol.
A **monument** can be very tall. It's a national symbol
A **memorial** helps us to recall. It's a national symbol.
Patriotic symbols show our love and our dedication
To the country we call home—the symbols of our nation.

Scaffolding the Content

Preview the Lesson

• During **Teach**, pp. 290–295
• 30 minutes

Point to the lesson title, and have students read it with you. Check whether students know the meaning of *nation* and *symbol*. You might write *The United States* on the board, and ask students if it is a nation or a symbol. Agree that it is the name of our nation, or country. Then say the names of objects, and ask students to find examples in the lesson. For example:

- Say *eagle*, and write it on the board. Ask students to find an image of an eagle in the lesson.

- Say *bell*, write it on the board, and ask students to find an image of a bell in the lesson.

- Repeat the procedure with the words *monument* and *memorial*. Suggest that students look at captions and labels to help them.

Modify Instruction

Now help students to explore the symbols more fully. Reproduce and pass out the blackline master page. Briefly review what a patriotic symbol is, then continue.

1. **Our Nation's Symbols** Ask students to identify the first symbol described in the lesson—the flag. Have students describe the flag in words or through hand motions. Then ask students to draw and label a flag in the top circle of their webs. Have students draw and label a bald eagle and the Liberty Bell in the two side circles of the web. Invite students to describe an eagle, and tell why it is a good symbol.

2. **A City of Monuments** Ask students where these monuments and memorials are, and agree that it is Washington, D.C. Ask students what is special about Washington, D.C., and agree that it is the capital of the United States. Then say *monument,* and have students point to the Washington Monument in the picture. Say: *George Washington was the first president of the United States, a long time ago.* Have students point to the various memorials on the pages, and point out which ones honor presidents and which ones honor people who fought in wars. Have students draw and label monuments and memorials on their webs. Ask students why we build monuments.

3. **Words of Patriotism** Have students find the word *anthem* in the text, and ask them to recall what an anthem is. Point to the picture of Francis Scott Key, and ask students who he might be. Agree that he wrote the words for the anthem for the United States, which is called "The Star-Spangled Banner." Finally, see if students can recite the Pledge of Allegiance. Ask students to write *anthem* and *pledge* on their webs. Ask students why an anthem like the "Star-Spangled Banner" is a good way to show patriotism.

Extend

• After **Teach**, pp. 290–295
• 15 minutes

Assign to each group member a symbol they learned about in the lesson. Ask each student to draw the symbol, and cut it out. On the back of the cutout, have students write a few words or sentences about it. Combine students' cutouts into a symbol mobile.

© Harcourt

Name _____ Date _____

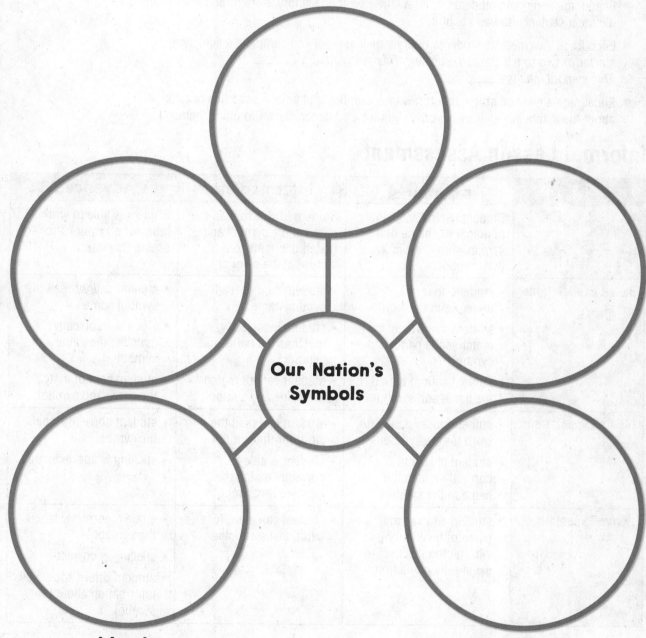

Symbols of Our Nation

Our Nation's Symbols

Words of Patriotism

Monuments and Memorials

School-Home Connection Invite students to take their graphic organizers home. Tell students to look around their home for any of the symbols they have drawn, or for any new symbols they see. Ask students to add the new symbols to the web. Encourage students to ask for help from their families.

© Harcourt

Apply and Assess

Draw a Symbol

Review the symbols from the lesson. Then ask each student to draw the patriotic symbol that they find the most interesting or that they like the most. Below the drawings, encourage students to write a sentence that tells about the symbol.

• During **Close**, p. 295
• 30 minutes

- Encourage beginning students to draw their symbol, identify it orally, and then dictate a sentence to you about it.
- Encourage intermediate students to draw their symbol and complete a sentence starter or two to tell about it, such as: *This symbol is* _____. *This symbol means* _____.
- Encourage advanced students to draw their symbol, and write a sentence or two about the symbol in their own words, without a sentence starter to guide them.

Informal Lesson Assessment

	Beginning	Intermediate	Advanced
Task	Student listens and is able to match the name of a symbol with the picture of that symbol.	Student is able to read the name of the symbol and match the name to a picture of the symbol.	Student is able to write a label for a symbol after seeing its picture.
Below Expectations	• student does not understand the word • student incorrectly matches the name and symbol • student cannot match the name and symbol	• student cannot read the symbol name • student incorrectly matches the name and symbol • student cannot match the name and symbol	• student cannot read the symbol name • student incorrectly matches the name and symbol • student cannot match the name and symbol
Meets Expectations	• student understands the word for the symbol • student is able to correctly match the name to the symbol	• student can read the word for the symbol • student is able to correctly match the name to the symbol	• student correctly labels the symbol • spelling is approximate
Above Expectations	• student can say the name of the symbol, without the teacher saying the name first	• student can identify additional symbols	• student correctly labels the symbol • spelling is correct • student offers additional information about the symbol

© Harcourt

Build Background

Access Prior Knowledge

Write the word *government* on the board, and see whether students can recognize and read it. Ask them to explain the word. List key words students suggest, such as: *lead, make laws, rule,* and *president.* Then have students tell what they know about the United States government. Say the name of each branch, and ask students to supply a simple word about it. Then ask students whether they think all countries have governments like this, and exchange ideas.

- Before **Introduce**, p. 300
- 20 minutes

Lesson Vocabulary

Hold up the textbook, and read the lesson title with the group. Say: *I am going to write some government words on the board. Practice saying them. They are in the lesson.* Then write **Parliament, prime minister,** and **constitutional monarchy** on the board. Say these words with the group several times. Use the word cards for reinforcement. Show students the cards, and help them practice recognizing the words from the board in a different context.

Additional Vocabulary Canada's government has a Cabinet of Ministers. Say the word *cabinet,* and ask students to point out a cabinet in the room, such as a file cabinet. Then explain that another meaning of *cabinet* is a group of people who work with a leader. Review other words or phrases in the margin in the context of the lesson, and have students make their own sentences.

branches
Cabinet of Ministers
goods
minister

Cognates As students read the lesson, you may wish to point out cognates such as: **constitutional/constitucional, monarchy/monarquía, Parliament/ parlamento, prime minister/primer/-a ministro/-a.**

Build Fluency

Read aloud the following rhyme, and point out the words that sound alike. Return to the chant throughout the lesson to help develop vocabulary, summarizing skills, and reinforce lesson content.

Mexico has a government
 That is much like ours.
It has three branches that can rule
 And a president with certain powers.
Canada has a government
 That is a little different.
Instead of a Senate, they have a **Parliament**
 And a **prime minister,** not a president.
The Asian country of Bhutan
 Is very different from ours.
It's a **constitutional monarchy,**
 So the king there shares power.

© Harcourt

Scaffolding the Content

Preview the Lesson

Explain that in this lesson, students will learn about different kinds of governments.

- During **Teach**, pp. 300–303
- 20 minutes

- First, ask students to define *neighbor*. You might have students name students who are their neighbors in class; *I sit next to Ana. Ana is my neighbor.* Then ask students which countries are neighbors of the United States. Show students a map of the world. Ask them to find the United States, Mexico, and Canada on the map. Ask students if they think Mexico and Canada are our neighbors.

- Next, have students study the map, and ask them to find Bhutan. Say: *Is Bhutan our neighbor?* Agree that Bhutan is not a neighbor of the United States. It is in Asia, between China and India in the Himalayan Mountains. Ask students whether they think Bhutan and the United States are similar.

Modify Instruction

Pass out copies of the blackline master page. Read the headings with students. Ask which countries listed are neighbors of the United States. Ask: *Which country is in Asia?* Tell students they will write or draw information about the governments of these countries on their blackline masters.

1 **Neighboring Governments** Have students skim the text on page 300 to find key words about Mexico's government. Have students identify the type of leader (president) and government (executive, legislative, and judicial branches) Mexico has. Tell students to write this information in their charts. Ask students whether this government is similar to or different from the United States government. (similar) Continue with the information about Canada on page 301. Ask students to identify Canada's leader (prime minister) and government branches (Parliament and Cabinet of Ministers). Ask students whether this government is similar to, or different from, the government of the United States.

2 **Bhutan's Government** Help students locate key words and phrases about Bhutan's government. Ask them which word tells about Bhutan's leader (king, monarch). Who is this? Have students write about Bhutan's leader on the chart. Then have students write down such phrases as *constitutional monarchy, National Assembly,* and *Council of Ministers* in the Branches box. Help students compare and contrast this government with that of the United States with such sentences as: *The United States has a leader called a president. Bhutan has a leader called a king.*

Extend

Have students name other countries that they know or that interest them. Help students research the type of government in these countries. Invite small groups of students to complete a chart like the one on the blackline master page to tell about and compare the governments.

- After **Teach**, pp. 300–303
- 20 minutes

© Harcourt

Name _____ Date _____

DIRECTIONS Fill in this chart to tell about the leaders and branches of different governments.

Governments of the World

Country	Leader	Branches
Mexico		
Canada		
Bhutan		

School-Home Connection Tell students to take their charts home to share with their families. Have students show their families the locations of Mexico, Canada, and Bhutan on a map. Suggest that students also explain how these governments are alike and different from the United States government.

© Harcourt

Unit 4, Chapter 8, Lesson 5

Success for English Learners ▪ 123

Apply and Assess

Write a Paragraph

Point out to students that this lesson gives details about three different world governments and shows how these governments are alike and different. Help students compare the governments.

• During Close, p. 303
• 20 minutes

- Beginning students should express their ideas orally as you write them down. You might say the name of one country, and have students tell you key words about it.

- Provide intermediate students with a sentence starter, such as: *The leader of Canada is the _____. The leader of Bhutan is the _____.*

- Challenge advanced students to write complete sentences that compare the governments of these three countries.

Informal Lesson Assessment

	Beginning	Intermediate	Advanced
Task	Student names the country when provided with a key word about its government.	Student reads a key word or phrase about a government and identifies the country.	Student writes the country's name after hearing clues about its government.
Below Expectations	• student does not understand the key word • student is unable to identify the country	• student cannot read the word • student does not understand the word • student cannot identify the country	• student does not understand the clues • student cannot identify the country • student cannot write the country's name
Meets Expectations	• student understands the key word • student identifies the country	• student can read the word and understand it • student can name the correct country	• student understands the clues • student correctly writes the country's name
Above Expectations	• student understands the key word • student identifies the country in a complete sentence	• student identifies the country in a complete sentence • student offers other information about that country's government	• student correctly writes the country's name • student writes a complete sentence about the country and its government

Developing Academic Language

Throughout this unit, students will be asked to look for cause-and-effect relationships. Students can better comprehend historical events when they understand these relationships and the sentence structures and vocabulary that signal them.

Introduce Cause and Effect

Set up a short tower of blocks or other objects on a table. Show students a ball, and act out rolling it down the table. Ask: *What's going to happen?* Invite students to express through words or gestures what will happen. Confirm their ideas by rolling the ball and knocking down the tower.

• Before **Cause and Effect**, p. 316
• 25 minutes

Tell students you just described a cause-and-effect relationship. Explain that a **cause** is something that makes something else happen. An **effect** is what happens because of the cause. Ask students whether rolling the ball toward the blocks was a cause or an effect (cause). Then ask them what word they would use to describe the blocks falling down (effect).

Suggest different ways to explain what happened: *The blocks fell down because the ball hit them. The ball hit the blocks, so they fell down. The ball hit the blocks and, as a result, the blocks fell down.* Tell students that certain words signal cause-and-effect relationships: *because, so, as a result, therefore.*

Practice

Write the following sentence frames on the board. Stand up textbooks on your desk and gently push them over with your hand. Work together to list the causes and effects of standing up and pushing down the textbooks.

I pushed the textbooks, so _____.

The textbooks fell down because _____.

Because _____, the textbooks stood up on my desk.

I stood up the textbooks on my desk. Then, I _____.

Apply

Write a simple cause-and-effect paragraph on the board. For example, describe effects of today's weather or what happens when students do not follow rules. Have students copy the chart below on a separate sheet of paper. Help students find causes and effects in the paragraph on the board and write them down. Gradually provide less help until students can work independently.

Cause	Effects
1. _____	1. _____
2. _____	2. _____
3. _____	3. _____

Build Background

Access Prior Knowledge

Begin by sharing information about a place you have lived before.
Say: *I lived in _____. I moved to _____.* Use gestures to convey
moving. Point to a map, and move your hand from one town to another as
you say *moving.* Invite students to share where they have moved from.
Have them echo the sentence, and fill in the words with their former and
new communities: *I lived in _____. I moved to _____.* Ask students
to name reasons for moving, and list them on the board.

• Before **Introduce**, p. 324
• 20 minutes

Lesson Vocabulary

Give each student the vocabulary cards for **opportunity, prejudice,** and
migrate. Then hold up the word card for *opportunity,* and say: *People move for
new opportunities. An opportunity is a chance to do something new.* Tell students
that in class they have opportunities to learn. Then hold up the word card for
prejudice. Ask students if they are familiar with this word, and explain that
having a prejudice means to not like someone because of their culture.
Finally, hold up the card for *migrate.* Say: *Migrate means to move from one place
to another.* As you say the meaning, walk from one end of the space to the
other, or use your map and gestures to indicate moving. Say simple phrases
that define each word, and have students hold up the card with its definition.

Additional Vocabulary Students might confuse the word *race* on page 325
with a competition. Explain that *race* can also mean a person's culture.
Preview page 325, and have students read the word race in the sentence.
Point out that the word is in the same sentence with *prejudice,* and have
students recall what they learned about prejudice. Review other words
or phrases in the margin in the context of the lesson, and have students make
their own sentences.

faced	moving
homelands	officers
immigrants	race
mild	settled

Cognates As students read the lesson, you may wish to point out cognates such
as: **apartment/apartamento, immigrant/inmigrante, migrate/migrar, migration/
migración, million/millón, opportunity/oportunidad, passport/pasaporte.**

Build Fluency

Read aloud the following chant, and
point out the words that sound alike.
Return to the chant throughout the
lesson to help develop vocabulary,
cause and effect skills, and reinforce
lesson content.

New **opportunity,** new opportunity,
People **migrate** to find a new opportunity.
Better education, better education,
People migrate to find a better education.
Jobs and more freedoms, jobs and more freedoms,
People migrate to find jobs and more freedoms.
It's not always easy, it's not always easy.
People might face **prejudice.** It's not always easy.

© Harcourt

Scaffolding the Content

Preview the Lesson

Write the word *immigrant* on the board, and say it for the group. Invite students to say it with you. Ask students whether this word is familiar and if they know what it means. Then have students view the first heading in the lesson, and ask them to point to the word *immigrants*. Looking at the photograph, ask students whether the meaning of immigrant is any clearer. Using a map and gestures to indicate moving, say: *Immigrants are people who move. Immigrants move from one country to another.* Tell students they will learn about immigrants in the United States.

• During **Teach**, pp. 324–329
• 30 minutes

Modify Instruction

Use the flow chart on the blackline master page to help students understand why people move to new places.

A Nation of Immigrants Have students recall what a nation is, and then ask which nation the heading talks about. Agree that it talks about the United States; the United States is often called a *nation of immigrants.* Encourage students to explain why. Point out the map on page 325. Agree that it shows different places around the world where people lived before they came to the United States. Have students write some of these places in the top box of the flow chart. Ask students where these people moved to, following the arrows on the chart. Have them write *The United States* in the middle box. Then ask students to turn back to page 324. Help them scan the text to find the reasons people moved to the United States, and tell them to write these ideas in the last box. Tell students to title this flow chart "A Nation of Immigrants."

Beginning New Lives Ask students how this heading might be related to immigrants. Let students communicate ideas, and then agree that when people move to a new place, they start a new life. Point out Ellis Island and Angel Island on a United States map. Explain that these were the first places many immigrants went when they came to the United States. Then many immigrants moved to different parts of the country.

Migration in the United States Have students notice how *migration* and *immigration* are similar. (You might cover the initial *im* to guide them.) Have students recall the word *migration* from the "Lesson Vocabulary" activity, and then ask what this heading might mean. Give students another copy of the flow chart. Ask them to title this chart "The Great Migration." Point out the picture, and explain that during the Great Migration, many African Americans left rural areas, which had few jobs. They moved to cities, which had many jobs. Have students summarize these ideas in the three boxes of the chart.

Extend

Give each student a file folder. Tell students to pretend the folder is a suitcase. (You might bring in a suitcase as an example.) Tell students to draw pictures of things they would take with them if they moved to another place. Have them write sentences telling why they would take these things, and put the drawings and sentences in their "suitcases."

• After **Teach**, pp. 324–329
• 20 minutes

© Harcourt

Name _____ Date _____

DIRECTIONS Write information in the flow chart to tell about people who move to new places.

Moving to New Places

Title: _____

Where Did They Come From?

↓

Where Did They Move?

↓

Why Did They Move?

 School-Home Connection Encourage students to share their flow charts with their families. Tell students to create another flow chart on a separate sheet of paper. Encourage students to complete this flow chart to tell their family's story of immigration, if their family is willing.

Apply and Assess

Write a Diary Entry

Write the word *diary* on the board, and have students read it with you. If possible, display a real diary. Ask students what a diary is, and agree that it is a book people write in to remember each day. Point to the picture of the children on page 324, and ask students what these children might be thinking as they come to the United States. Tell students they will write a diary that tells what they might think is hard about moving.

• During **Close**, p. 329
• 40 minutes

- Let beginning students dictate their ideas to you. Record their ideas, and read them back to them.

- Intermediate students can work with partners to exchange ideas and help each other write sentences for their diary entries.

- Advanced students should be encouraged to write the diary entries on their own and to include information from the lesson.

Informal Lesson Assessment

	Beginning	Intermediate	Advanced
Task	Students draw pictures to show why people move to new places.	Students write an answer to the question: *Why do people move to new places?*	Students write a paragraph to answer the question: *Why do people move to new places?*
Below Expectations	• student does not understand the question • student cannot answer the question • student answers the question incorrectly	• student does not understand the question • student cannot answer the question • student answers the question incorrectly	• student does not understand the question • student cannot answer the question • student answers the question incorrectly
Meets Expectations	• student understands the question • student answers the question correctly, giving one reason	• student understands the question • student answers the question correctly, giving one reason • spelling is approximate	• student answers the question correctly • spelling is approximate • sentence construction is adequate; several mistakes
Above Expectations	• student answers the question correctly, providing several reasons	• student answers the question correctly and gives several reasons • spelling is correct	• student's paragraph is written correctly • spelling is correct • information is correct and interesting

Build Background

Access Prior Knowledge

Write the word *culture* on the board, and say it with the group. Have
students say words that tell about culture, such as *country, different, food,
music*. Invite students to draw objects from their culture, such as a special
food, clothing, or musical instrument. Provide time for students to share
their drawings. Say: *Good! You share your drawings. You share your cultures!*

• Before **Introduce**, p. 332
• 20 minutes

Lesson Vocabulary

Display the following sentences. Have pairs of students work together to say
or write a definition for each vocabulary word based on context clues.
Discuss the words that provide context clues. Students can look the
vocabulary words up in the Glossary to verify their meanings.

1 A **diverse** community has people from many different cultures.

2 We have a **multicultural** classroom. We have people from
   South America, Africa, and Asia.

3 On birthdays, our **custom** is to sing "Happy Birthday."

4 The town's July 4 parade is a **tradition** we enjoy every year.

5 Food from different **ethnic groups** has become popular in
   the United States.

Additional Vocabulary Share with students the words for ethnic groups
listed in the margin. Explain that students will see these words in the
text. Write the country names on the board, and have students match
each country with its ethnic group.

Cognates As students read the lesson, you may wish to point out
cognates such as: **diversity/diversidad, ethnic/étnico/-a,
multicultural/multicultural, tradition/tradición.**

African	Irish
Asian	Italian
Caribbean	Mexican
Chinese	Polish
Czech	Thai
Greek	Vietnamese

Build Fluency

Read aloud the following rhyme,
and point out the words that
sound alike. Return to the chart
throughout the lesson to help
develop vocabulary, cause and
effect skills, and reinforce lesson
content. This rhyme can loosely be
sung to the tune of "Pop! Goes the
Weasel."

A community can be **diverse**
With lots of different cultures.
We call this **multicultural**
And enjoy all these cultures.
All people have their own cultures,
Their **customs** and **traditions.**
They all live in a community
And share their traditions.
What makes up an **ethnic group?**
People of one culture.
They share their customs and traditions.
They have the same culture.

© Harcourt

Scaffolding the Content

Preview the Lesson

Tell students they will learn about the people who make up three communities in the United States. To preview the chapter, introduce students to these communities.

• During **Teach**, pp. 332–337
• 40 minutes

- **Washington, D.C.** Have students share what they know about Washington, D.C., and then locate it on a map. Write *Chinatown* and *Adams Morgan* on the board. Explain that these are neighborhoods in Washington, D.C. Have students repeat these sentences: *Washington, D.C., is multicultural. People from many ethnic groups live here. They share their cultures.*

- **Cleveland, Ohio** Locate Cleveland on a map for students. Invite volunteers to share what they know about this city. Say these sentences for students to repeat: *Cleveland, Ohio, is multicultural. Many ethnic groups live here. They share their cultures.*

- **Chamblee, Georgia** Show students the town's location on a map. Ask students to share anything they know about Georgia, and then have them repeat these sentences: *Chamblee, Georgia, is multicultural. Many ethnic groups live here. They share their cultures.*

Modify Instruction

Give each student three copies of the blackline master on the next page. Explain that the charts will help them understand how different ethnic groups share their cultures.

1. **Washington, D.C.** Have students write *Washington, D.C.* in the top box. In the middle boxes, have them write the names of ethnic groups that live in this city: Chinese, Latin American, Caribbean, African, and Asian. Then ask students what these groups might contribute to the neighborhood. In the bottom box, have students write *shops* and *restaurants*, and draw pictures to show they know what the words mean.

2. **Cleveland, Ohio** Have students write *Cleveland, Ohio* in the top box of another flow chart. See if students can find the names of ethnic groups that live in this city. Have students write *African American, Italian, Czech, Irish*, and *Polish* in the middle row of boxes. Ask: *How do they share their cultures?* Have students write *Cleveland Cultural Garden* in the bottom box. Ask students why this name is a good name for a place that honors different cultures. Ask: *What is a garden?* Have them write *African American Museum* in this box, too. Review what a museum is.

3. **Chamblee, Georgia** Follow the same procedure with the section on Chamblee, Georgia. Ask: *How do they share their cultures?* Students can write *restaurants, traditional foods, bookstore,* and *music store* in the bottom box.

Extend

Make a "cultural garden." Tell each student to draw and cut out the outline of a flower, and attach it to a craft stick. In the flower's center, students should draw one way an ethnic group can share its culture, such as a museum or special shop. Arrange the flowers in a class cultural garden by poking the sticks in the bottom of an inverted box.

• After **Teach**, pp. 332–337
• 15 minutes

© Harcourt

Name _____ Date _____

DIRECTIONS Fill in this flow chart to show how different groups share their cultures.

Sharing Cultures

Title: _____

City

↓ ↓ ↓ ↓ ↓ ↓

Ethnic Groups						

↓ ↓ ↓ ↓ ↓ ↓

How They Share Their Cultures

 School-Home Connection Encourage students to talk with their families about their customs and traditions. Tell students to ask their families how they share their customs and traditions with others. Have students draw a picture that shows what they learn, and share with the class.

© Harcourt

Apply and Assess

Make a Bulletin Board

Set up a bulletin board so that it resembles the flow chart on the previous page. If a bulletin board is not available, give students another flow chart to complete. Ask them to write the name of their community in the top box and any ethnic groups they know about in the middle boxes. Discuss with students how ethnic groups in their community share their cultures. For example, perhaps the neighborhood has an ethnic festival or restaurants.

• During **Close**, p. 337
• 30 minutes

- Beginning learners should name their community orally or in writing. Direct students to the names of ethnic groups, and then ask them to draw how the groups share their cultures.

- Intermediate students should work with partners to tell about how community groups share their cultures.

- Advanced students can complete the bulletin board or flow chart on their own.

Informal Lesson Assessment

	Beginning	Intermediate	Advanced
Task	Students name and illustrate one way that ethnic groups share their cultures.	Students illustrate one way that groups share their cultures, and write a caption for their illustration.	Students write a paragraph that compares the different ways groups share their cultures.
Below Expectations	• student does not understand the task • student cannot name any ways that groups share their cultures • drawing does not reflect the task	• student does not understand the task • drawing does not reflect the task • caption does not reflect the topic or the illustration	• student does not understand the task • student cannot recall how groups share their cultures • writing does not reflect task
Meets Expectations	• student is able to name a way that groups share their cultures • drawing reflects the task	• drawing reflects the task • caption reflects the drawing • spelling is approximate	• student recalls several ways that groups share their cultures • spelling is approximate • sentence construction is adequate; sentences have many mistakes
Above Expectations	• student writes a caption that tells about the illustration	• spelling is correct • sentences are properly constructed	• spelling is correct • sentences are properly constructed • sentences are interesting

© Harcourt

Build Background

Access Prior Knowledge

Write the word *heritage* on the board, and say it for the group. Draw a circle around *heritage*, and create a word web from it. Say other words that are related to heritage, such as *culture, custom, tradition,* and *beliefs.* Have students say each word with you, and ask them to describe what the words mean. They may provide examples of customs or traditions they know. Explain that all these things make up a person's heritage.

• Before **Introduce**, p. 338
• 20 minutes

Lesson Vocabulary

Add three circles to the word web from "Access Prior Knowledge." Write **landmark, statue,** and **holiday** in the circles. Point to each word, and say it with the group. Encourage students to define the words, helping as needed. Say: *A holiday is a special day. What holidays do you know?* In the circle, write suggestions. For *statue,* show students a picture of a statue. Say: *A statue often honors a person. What statues do you know?* List ideas in the circle. Finally, help students understand *landmark.* Ask what the word *land* means. Then ask what it might mean to *mark* the *land* (to make part of the land easy to recognize). Suggest a community landmark as an example. In the circle, list other landmarks that students name.

Additional Vocabulary Write *human feature* on the board, and read it with the group. Explain that a human feature is a landmark made by a human, or person. Say: *A statue is a* human feature. *What are some others?* Review other words or phrases in the margin in the context of the lesson, and have students make their own sentences.

Cognates As students read the lesson, you may wish to point out cognates such as: **celebrate/celebrar, common/común, image/imagen, independence/independencia, island/isla.**

belonging	served
common	set aside
huddled masses	sign
human feature	well-known
make up	yearning

Build Fluency

Read aloud the following rhyme, and point out the words that sound alike. Return to the chant throughout the lesson to help develop vocabulary, cause and effect skills, and reinforce lesson content. This rhyme can loosely be sung to "Yankee Doodle Dandy."

People of many different cultures can live in one community
With different traditions, beliefs, and ethnic **holidays.**
They also share national holidays and **landmarks** in the community.
They share a common bond in many other ways.

What do we all have in common? What do we all share?
We share our American heritage! You see it everywhere!
Citizens and **statues**, landmarks we are fond of
Are the things that we all share and that we all love.

© Harcourt

Scaffolding the Content

Preview the Lesson

• During **Teach**, pp. 338–341
• 30 minutes

Say the phrase *our American heritage,* and ask students to repeat it. You might have them recite the chant to listen for the words there. Write the phrase on the board as you say it, and have students find this phrase in the text (it is the lesson title). Then point to pictures in the lesson, and have students say: *These things are part of our American heritage.* Tell students to draw pictures of objects in their heritage, and ask them what they represent. Guiding them to use the words *culture, custom, tradition,* and *beliefs.* Tell students they will learn about things that make up, or are part of, our American heritage.

Modify Instruction

Pass out copies of the blackline master. Have students recognize and read the page title, and then read the question in the top box. Tell students that as they complete the chart, they will gather information to help answer this question.

1 **American Landmarks** Encourage students to find this heading on their charts. Ask students to recall the meaning of *landmark.* Then ask whether they recognize the two landmarks on pages 338 and 339. Point to each landmark, and say: *This landmark is part of our American heritage.* Then ask students whether it honors a person, an idea, or an event. Have students illustrate and write about each landmark on their charts.

2 **National Holidays** Have students find this heading on their charts. Have students recall the meaning of *holiday.* Ask them to write *Celebrate People* next to #1. Help students convey *celebrate,* acting out its meaning by clapping, waving, or cheering. Point to the picture of the soldier, and say: *This man is a veteran. He fought in a war. We celebrate veterans on Veterans Day.* Have students write *Veterans Day* and draw a picture of who it honors. Point to the picture of Martin Luther King, Jr. on the banner. Say: *This man is Martin Luther King, Jr. He worked for freedom. We celebrate him on Martin Luther King Day.* Have students write *Martin Luther King Day* and draw a picture of who it honors on their charts. Display a picture of a United States president. Say: *This man was president. We celebrate American presidents on Presidents' Day.* Have students write *Presidents' Day* and who it honors on their charts. For #2, ask students to write *Celebrate History.* Have students find the date in the text, and say: *The Fourth of July celebrates American history.* Have students write *Fourth of July,* and draw pictures to show what it celebrates.

Extend

• After **Teach**, pp. 338–341
• 20 minutes

Work with the group to make a heritage collage. Have students draw pictures to represent landmarks and holidays from the lesson or their own knowledge. Arrange students' drawings in a collage on a sheet of poster paper. Point to the pictures, and have students say words or phrases about them.

© Harcourt

Name _____ Date _____

DIRECTIONS Fill in the chart to show the holidays and landmarks that make up our American heritage.

Our American Heritage

What Makes Up Our American Heritage?

American Landmarks

Landmark	What It Honors
1.	
2.	

National Holidays

Holidays	Who It Honors
1.	
2.	
3.	

 School-Home Connection Have students take their charts home and share them with their families. Tell students to read the question in the top box, and answer it by reading the chart. Have students ask their families what else they could add to their charts.

© Harcourt

Apply and Assess

Draw a Landmark

Ask students to name their community and state. Write both names on the board. Then brainstorm with students a list of landmarks that they might see in their community or state. Guide students' ideas as necessary. If you have pictures of community or state landmarks, share them with the group. Then ask students to choose one landmark to draw.

• During **Close**, p. 341
• 30 minutes

- Beginning students should draw their landmark, and identify it orally. You might have students use this sentence frame: _____ *makes up our American heritage.*

- Intermediate students should draw their landmark, and be encouraged to write a label for it. They might complete the sentence: _____ *makes up our American heritage.*

- Advanced students should draw their landmark, and be encouraged to write a few sentences to tell about how it makes up our American heritage.

Informal Lesson Assessment

	Beginning	Intermediate	Advanced
Task	Students draw and identify one landmark or holiday that makes up our American heritage.	Students draw and write a caption about one holiday or landmark that makes up our American heritage.	Students draw and write two to three sentences that tell about several landmarks or holidays that make up our American heritage.
Below Expectations	• student does not understand the task • drawing does not reflect the task • student cannot identify the drawing	• student does not understand the task • drawing does not reflect the task • caption does not reflect the drawing	• student can only recall one thing to draw • writing does not reflect the drawing
Meets Expectations	• student understands the task • drawing is on task • student can identify the drawing orally	• drawing reflects the task • caption reflects the drawing • spelling is approximate	• student draws several things • spelling is approximate • sentence construction is adequate; sentences have many mistakes
Above Expectations	• student can draw, identify, and write the name of an American landmark or holiday	• spelling is correct • sentences are properly constructed	• spelling is correct • sentences are properly constructed • sentences are interesting

Build Background

Access Prior Knowledge

Invite students to share songs in their own languages or from their cultures. You might also share an ethnic folktale from a book. Write the word *express* on the board, and explain that it means to tell about. Say: *We express our cultures in songs. We express our cultures in stories.* Ask: *How else might you express your culture?* Let students offer ideas orally or through gestures, and list them on the board.

• Before **Introduce**, p. 348
• 20 minutes

Lesson Vocabulary

Hold up a large storybook, and have students identify it. Say: *Some books tell stories. Stories are called* **literature.** *We express our cultures in literature.* Write *literature* on a sticky note, place it on the book, and say it with the group. Then say: *There are different kinds of literature. They all express cultures. Some kinds of literature are* **myths, fables, folktales,** *and* **legends.** Display examples of these genres, and have students use labeled sticky notes to identify them. Then say: *Folk song,* and have students sing a simple folk song. Write *folk song* on the board. Say: *We also express our cultures in folk songs.* Write **worship** on the board, and make a praying hand motion. Ask students to show through gestures how they worship. Say: *We also express our cultures in worship.*

Additional Vocabulary In the previous lesson, the words *made up* meant to contribute to, as in, "All these things made up our American heritage." In this lesson, the words *made up* describe an imaginary story or something that is not true. Use context clues to explain the remaining words in the margin, and let students create their own sentences.

beat	rhythm
made up	storyteller
nickname	teachings
oral	written
perform	

Cognates As students read the lesson, you may wish to point out cognates such as: **creativity/creatividad, expression/expresión, legend/leyenda, literature/literatura, mural/mural, oral/oral.**

Build Fluency

Read aloud the following rhyme, and point out the words that sound alike. Return to the chant throughout the lesson to help develop vocabulary, cause and effect skills, and reinforce lesson content.

Express your culture! Tell your story!
If you are shy, sing without worry!
Literature means stories to tell,
Myths and **fables,** and **legends** as well.
Folktales and **folk songs** are traditions
Passed on down through generations.
Worship is something we must mention,
It's another cultural expression.
Dance! Paint! Build something, too.
Express your culture, express you!

© Harcourt

Scaffolding the Content

● Preview the Lesson

Pass out four copies of the blackline master from the following page to each student. Help students complete them as you provide an overview of the lesson. First, have students write the lesson title in the center circle. Then ask them to scan the lesson to find the main headings: *Written and Oral Traditions, The Arts, Religions.* Ask students to write these headings in an outer circle of the web. Then have students look closely at the pictures and study the people. Ask whether they can find another expression of culture (clothing). Ask students to write *Clothing* in the fourth circle. Ask students what they already know about each of the headings. Tell them they will read about the many ways people express their culture.

• During **Teach**, pp. 348–353
• 20 minutes

Modify Instruction

Begin to explore the lesson, giving students a blank blackline master.

1 Written and Oral Traditions Tell students to write the heading and the word *literature* in the center circle of the web. Ask students what object could represent this topic (book), and have them draw this in the center circle. Have students find and recognize the boldfaced vocabulary words in the lesson, and ask them to write each word in a circle of the web. Then help students distinguish each type of story. Say that a myth is a story that people make up to explain the world. An example is Anansi the Spider, who is said to have created the sun, moon, and stars. A fable is a story in which animals speak and act like people. An example is the Tortoise and the Hare. A folktale is a story passed from one generation to the next. An example is the Japanese folktale about Urashima Taro. A legend is a made-up story about a real person, like Johnny Appleseed. Ask students if they know any myths, folklores, or legends.

2 The Arts On a fresh word web, tell students to write the section title in the center circle. Explain that the arts include literature, paintings, music, dance, and other things. Say: *Murals are large paintings on a wall,* and point to the picture on page 350. Say: *Folk songs express, or tell about, a culture.* Point to the pictures on pages 350 and 351, and say: *Dances are movements that go with music.* Let students dance beside their desks. Point to the pyramids on page 351, and say: *Architecture is the art of building.* Have students write and illustrate *mural, folk song, dance,* and *buildings* in the outer circles of their webs. Then have students write examples of each.

3 Religions On a third web, tell students to write *Religions* in the center circle, as well as the word *worship.* Ask students about their own religions. Find out where they worship and what customs they have. List the names of some religions. Repeat this sentence pattern for each religion, and have students write the religion and place of worship in a circle on their webs: _____ *worship in a* _____.

Extend

Invite students to contribute to a mural that tells about cultural expression. Ask each student to draw a picture that shows something they learned in this lesson. Have students write a caption for their drawings, too.

• After **Teach**, pp. 348–353
• 10 minutes

© Harcourt

Name _____ Date _____

DIRECTIONS How do people express their culture? Write about it in
the diagram below.

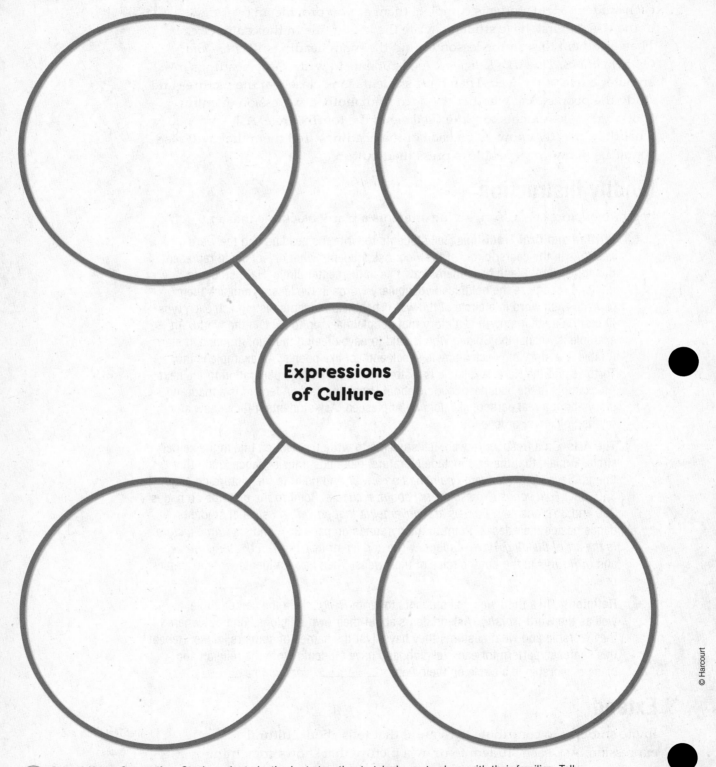

 School-Home Connection Staple each student's charts together to take home to share with their families. Tell
students to act out some of the cultural expressions shown on their webs. Then ask students to create another
web to show how their families express their cultures.

Apply and Assess

Write a Fable

Remind students that a fable is a story in which animals speak and act like people. Share a fable, either by memory or from a collection, to help them understand this genre. Solicit ideas from students about the features of a fable, such as the line *Once upon a time*, and so on. Ask students which animals are common in their community. The animals can be pets, forest animals, park animals, desert animals, and so on. Tell students to think of a story idea using these animals, and invite them to create a fable.

- During **Close**, p. 353
- 30 minutes

- Beginning students can illustrate a scene from their story and then use their picture as a prompt to tell about their animals.

- Intermediate students should illustrate a scene for their story and then write captions or short sentences to tell their story.

- Advanced students should write their stories independently, including dialogue between the animals, and then illustrate a scene.

Informal Lesson Assessment

	Beginning	Intermediate	Advanced
Task	Students pantomime ways that people express their cultures.	Students pantomime and talk about ways that people express their cultures.	Students choose one of three categories in the lesson (literature, arts, or religion) and tell how it expresses culture.
Below Expectations	• student does not understand the task • pantomime does not reflect cultural expression	• student does not understand the task • pantomime does not reflect cultural expression • language does not reflect pantomime	• student chooses inappropriate category • student cannot name forms of cultural expression • cultural expressions do not match category
Meets Expectations	• student understands the task • pantomime reflects cultural expression • student can orally identify the cultural expression	• pantomime reflects a form of cultural expression • language reflects the pantomime	• student correctly chooses one of the three categories • forms of cultural expressions are correct for that category • language is slightly halting, with mistakes
Above Expectations	• student can pantomime and orally identify expression • student can group it as literature, the arts, or religion	• pantomime and language tell about cultural expression • student speaks in clear, complete sentences	• category and expressions are correct • oral language is smooth • sentences are spoken correctly

Build Background

Access Prior Knowledge

Bring some party favors to class, or draw pictures of them on the board. Then ask students to say words related to these items, such as *party, holiday, festival, fun,* and *tradition.* Write *holiday* on the board, and ask students to name holidays they know. List students' ideas on the board.

• Before **Introduce**, p. 358
• 20 minutes

Lesson Vocabulary

Hold up the vocabulary card for the word **festival.** Read it to the group, and then invite students to read it with you. This word might sound familiar to students, so let students say words they associate with it. Guide students to such words as *big party, celebration, special day, many people, happy day,* and so on. Ask students why people might have a festival. To answer the question, let students draw pictures of a festival, and help them write a title that tells what the festival celebrates.

Additional Vocabulary The context of the word *falls* on page 360 might confuse students. Have students lift their arms and then let their arms "fall" to their desks. Agree that this is one meaning of the word *fall.* Then show students a calendar, and help students find a holiday noted there. Place the calendar on a flat surface, lift your arm, and have it "fall" on that date. Say: *This holiday falls on this day.* Review other words or phrases in the margin in the context of the lesson, and have students make their own sentences.

falls	meal
fireworks	messages
garden hose	week-long
grown	

Cognates As students read the lesson, you may wish to point out cognates such as: **calendar/calendario, celebration/celebración, crystal/cristal, decorate/decorar, festival/festival, music/música, religious/religioso/-a.**

Build Fluency

Read aloud the following rhyme, and point out the words that sound alike. Return to the rhyme throughout the lesson to help develop vocabulary, cause and effect skills, and reinforce lesson content. The rhyme can loosely be sung to the tune of "London Bridge Is Falling Down."

Holidays are special days, special days, special days!
Holidays are special days—have fun and celebrate.
Can you name some holidays, holidays, holidays?
Can you name some holidays? Here are some of them.
St. Patrick's Day, Kwanzaa, too, and New Year's Day, that's a few!
Can you name some holidays? Cinco de Mayo.
Holidays have **festivals,** festivals, festivals!
Holidays have festivals—everyone can come!
Parades and food and candles, too, traditions all, just a few!
Holidays have customs, too, of things we like to do.
Holidays are special days, we celebrate in special ways!
Holidays are special days—have fun and celebrate!

© Harcourt

Scaffolding the Content

Preview the Lesson

Invite students to view the photographs before exploring the lesson. Have students describe images they see in the photographs, such as colors, objects, shapes, and clothing. Also, have students try to identify the action taking place, accompanied by pantomimes. For example, on page 358, students can march at their desks, as if in a parade. Tell students that they will learn more about these festivals and celebrations as they explore the lesson.

• During **Teach**, pp. 358–361
• 20 minutes

Modify Instruction

Give each student a copy of the blackline master. Have them recognize and read the page title, matching it with the lesson title. Then begin exploring the lesson content.

1 **Cultural Holidays** Have students find this heading on their charts. Say the words *traditional cultural celebrations* slowly, so students can distinguish the words, and explain each word individually if needed. Then have students write *St. Patrick's Day* in one part of the circle, along with *Irish culture*. Ask a volunteer to tell about celebrating St. Patrick's Day if appropriate. In the next portion of the circle, have students write *Cinco de Mayo* and *Mexican Independence Day*. Ask students which country or culture celebrates these holidays, and have students write *Mexico* on their papers. Have students write key words to tell about each, such as *battle against France, freedom from Spain*. Finally, have students write *Kwanzaa* and *African Americans* in the last part of the circle. Ask volunteers to tell about celebrating Cinco de Mayo and Kwanzaa if appropriate. Have students write *celebrates community* in the circle. Encourage students to illustrate their charts using colors shown in the pictures.

2 **New Year's Day** Explore this part of the lesson in the same way. Have students write the culture associated with each new year celebration—American, Chinese, and Thai. Then have students write what is special about each celebration; for example: crystal ball and Times Square, New York City (American); students get red packets with money, dragon dances (Chinese); Songkran, April, throwing cold water on people (Thai). Encourage volunteers to share their experiences with these celebrations if appropriate. Encourage students to illustrate these ideas, using colors from the pictures.

Extend

Make a holiday scrapbook with the group. Assign, or let students choose, a holiday described in this lesson. Ask students to draw a picture to illustrate the holiday, and then have them write captions. Tell students to glue their pictures to colored construction paper for a background and to choose a color that matches the colors in the book photographs. Then combine students' pages with yarn to form a holiday book.

• After **Teach**, pp. 358–361
• 20 minutes

Name _____ Date _____

DIRECTIONS Use the circles below to show what you learned about cultural holidays and new year's holidays. Write information, and draw pictures in the circles below.

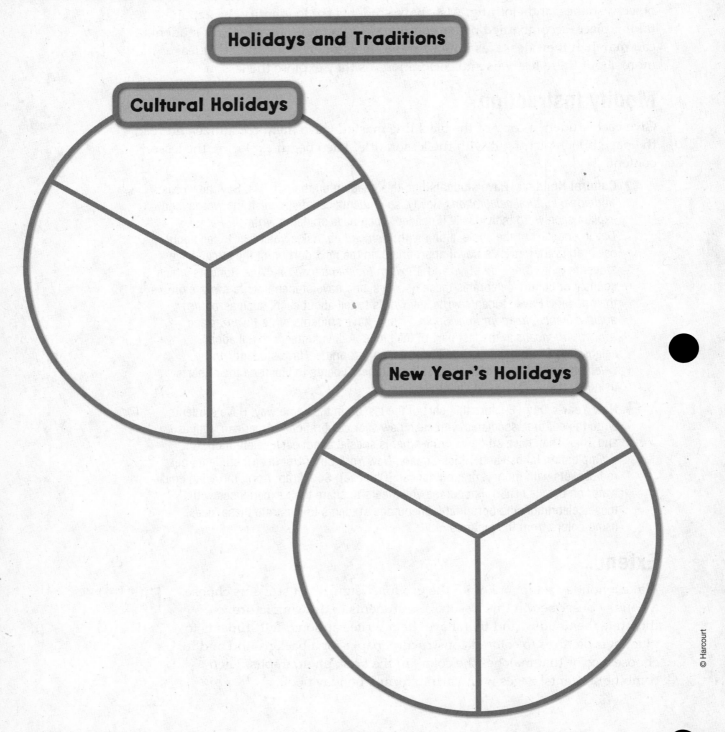

Holidays and Traditions

Cultural Holidays

New Year's Holidays

School-Home Connection Have students show their completed circle charts to their families to share information about these holidays and traditions. Tell students to ask their families what other holidays they could add to a different circle chart. Tell students to complete a third circle chart with help from their families and to share it with the class.

Apply and Assess

Write a Description

Explain that a description is writing that tells about colors and shapes and sounds and tastes; it is writing that tells what something is like. Read some simple descriptive writing to provide students with an example. Then brainstorm with students different holidays your community celebrates. Also brainstorm ways each holiday is celebrated. Ask students to choose one holiday to describe.

• During **Close**, p. 361
• 30 minutes

- Beginning students can dictate descriptive words to you about the holiday.

- Intermediate students can write simple descriptive sentences with the help of a partner.

- Challenge advanced students to write several sentences or a descriptive paragraph.

Informal Lesson Assessment

	Beginning	**Intermediate**	**Advanced**
Task	Students create an invitation to a holiday celebration discussed in the lesson. Invitations should convey in labels or pictures what the holiday celebrates.	Students create an invitation to a holiday celebration discussed in the lesson. Invitations should convey in phrases or short sentences what the holiday celebrates.	Students create an invitation to a holiday celebration discussed in the lesson. Invitations should convey in complete sentences what the holiday celebrates.
Below Expectations	• student does not understand the task • student cannot recall a holiday from lesson	• student does not understand the task • student cannot recall a holiday from lesson • card does not reflect the holiday	• student does not understand the task • student cannot recall a holiday from lesson • student cannot write about the holiday
Meets Expectations	• student understands the task • student chooses a holiday from the lesson • student's card reflects the holiday through simple pictures	• student recalls a holiday from lesson • student's card reflects the chosen holiday • spelling is approximate	• student recalls a holiday from lesson • student correctly writes about why the holiday is important • spelling and sentence structure need work
Above Expectations	• student's card reflects the chosen holiday • card communicates importance of holiday	• student's card reflects the holiday • spelling is correct	• information on card is correct • spelling and sentences are correct

© Harcourt

Build Background

Access Prior Knowledge

Help students recall the cultures they have already learned about (Chinese, African American, Irish, and so on). You might display pictures from previous lessons to prompt their memories. Then ask students how all the cultures are similar. Agree that people from these cultures live in the United States. They also live around the world. Explain that students are going to learn how all cultures are the same. They will also learn how cultures are different.

• Before **Introduce**, p. 362
• 20 minutes

Lesson Vocabulary

Write the words *culture* and *cultural* on the board. Ask volunteers to share the meaning of culture by pointing to photographs in the book about their own cultures. Explain that *cultural* describes something that is connected to culture. Write the word *identity* on the board, and say it several times with the group. Say: *Identity is a word that tells about you. Your identity is who you are.* Now write the two words side by side: **cultural identity.** Ask students what they think a person's cultural identity is. Agree that cultural identity is the things, or traits, that a culture has, or that people identify with. You might let students draw pictures of items that show their cultural identity.

Additional Vocabulary Write *similar* and *alike* on the board, each enclosed in a circle. In a square shape, write the word *different*. Point to *similar* and *alike*, and say: *These words mean the same thing.* Point to *different*, and say: *This word means not the same.* Review other words or phrases in the margin in the context of the lesson, and have students make their own sentences.

alike	spongy
close	traits
different	vegetables
native	

Cognates As children read the lesson, you may wish to point out cognates such as: **cultural/cultural, different/diferente, identity/identidad, practice/practicar.**

Build Fluency

Read aloud the following rhyme, and point out the words that sound alike. Return to the chant throughout the lesson to help develop vocabulary, cause and effect skills, and reinforce lesson content.

Our world has many countries, so look and you will see.
Our world has many cultures and **cultural identities.**
The foods we eat, the words we speak, the clothes we like to wear
Make up our cultural identity, which we proudly share!
From things we build to things we make, and songs we like to sing,
Our cultural identity includes all these special things.
Our world has many countries, so look and you will see.
Our world has many cultures—what's your cultural identity?

© Harcourt

Scaffolding the Content

Preview the Lesson

To help students identify how cultures are similar and different, have students turn to pages 364 and 365. Ask students to point out how the people in the pictures are the same. For example: They are all children; they are wearing interesting clothing; they appear on a map; a line on the map connects each child to a country.

Now ask students to explain how the people are different. For example: They are wearing different clothing; they live in different parts of the world; some are boys; some are girls.

Tell children that they will learn how cultures around the world are alike and different.

• During **Teach**, pp. 362–367
• 30 minutes

Modify Instruction

Reproduce three copies of the blackline master for each student. Give each student one copy to help students understand how cultures are alike and different.

❶ **Ways of Life** Write *Africa* and *Europe* on the board, and say the words with the group. Ask students what they know about these places, and agree that Europe and Africa are both continents. On their graphic organizers, have students write "Ways of Life" on the title line. Ask them to title one box *Africa* and the other box *Europe.* In the middle circle, they should write other ways these places are similar: 1. They both have about 700 million people; 2. They both have hundreds of culture groups; 3. People in both continents speak different languages; 4. People in both continents enjoy different foods. Make sure students understand that these ways of life are the same in Europe and Africa. Then turn to page 363. Tell students to write *Ethiopia* in the Africa box, and *Spain* in the Europe box. Guide students to write or draw what is special about each country in their boxes.

❷ **People of the World** As in the previous section, have children use their blackline masters to record what the children in these photos have in common: 1. People are proud of their own cultures. 2. They wear clothing to show their cultural identities. Have students write *cultural identity* in the center circle with other facts as you say: *All people have a cultural identity.* Let students choose two children to compare, drawing and writing ideas in the outer boxes.

❸ **Expressions of Culture** Pass out the third graphic organizer. Have students write the section heading on the title line. Explain that people of all cultures express their culture in special ways. Say: *All cultures have special architecture, or buildings, special music, and special dances. These are part of their cultural identity.* Now guide students to write what is special about Japanese architecture and Brazilian music and dance, writing and drawing their ideas in the outer boxes.

Extend

Provide the group with a children's atlas or gazetteer. Have students look up a country displayed on pages 364 and 365 that interests them. Tell students to study how these countries and cultures are the same and different from their own.

• After **Teach**, pp. 362–367
• 20 minutes

Name _____ Date _____

DIRECTIONS Listen to your teacher. Write information and draw pictures in the chart to show how two cultures are the same and different.

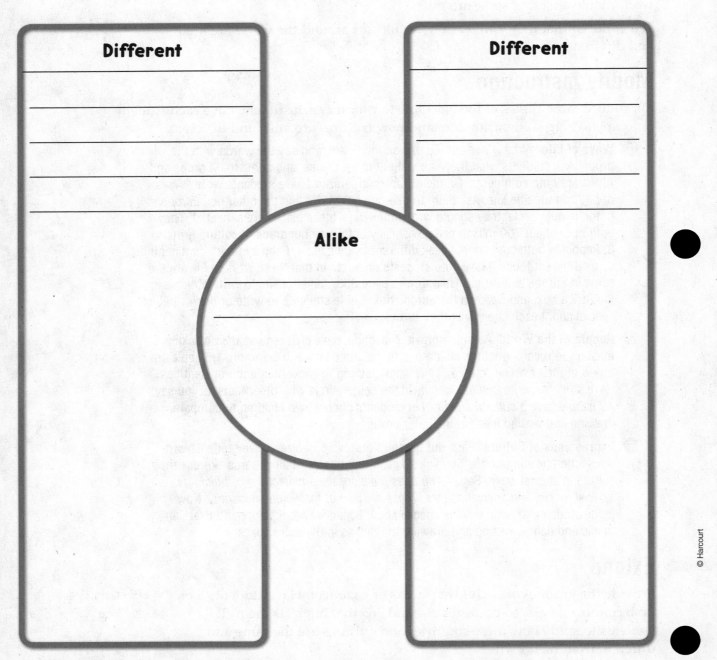

Cultures of the World

Section Title: _____

Different

Different

Alike

School-Home Connection Have students tell their families about the cultures they learned about. Then suggest that students compare their family's culture with those of a friend to discover how they are alike and different.

© Harcourt

Apply and Assess

Make a List

Write the term *cultural expressions* on the board. Students might confuse the word *expressions* with the word that means phrase or saying. Explain that in this lesson, the word *expressions* refers to different ways people express, or show, their culture; the ways do not have to be with words. Also show students examples of a list so they know what is expected of them.

• During **Close**, p. 367
• 30 minutes

- Beginning students can say the name of several types of cultural expression as you write them down. Allow students to refer to the photographs in the lesson for prompts, if needed.

- Intermediate students should refer to the photographs for prompts and try to write the words on their own.

- Advanced students should be encouraged to recall information without help from the book. Let students check their lists against the book text and photographs when they are finished.

Informal Lesson Assessment

	Beginning	Intermediate	Advanced
Task	Students view pages 364 and 365 and orally identify how the cultures or children are alike and different.	Students choose two cultures from the text and write how they are alike and different, using a sentence frame.	Students choose two cultures from the text and write a paragraph to explain how they are alike and different.
Below Expectations	• student does not understand the task • student is unable to express ideas orally • ideas expressed do not reflect the topic	• student does not understand prompt • student is unable to compare and contrast • student is unable to convey ideas through writing	• paragraph does not compare two cultures • paragraph compares two cultures, but ideas are incorrect • many mistakes in spelling and grammar
Meets Expectations	• student understands the task • student is able to express ideas orally • ideas tell how the children or cultures are alike and different	• student understands the prompt • student is able to compare and contrast • student conveys ideas through writing • approximate spelling	• paragraph compares two cultures • ideas are correct • spelling and grammar need work
Above Expectations	• ideas tell how the children or cultures are alike and different • student speaks in clear, complete sentences	• student conveys similarities and differences beyond the prompt • spelling is correct	• paragraph adequately compares and contrasts two cultures • spelling and grammar are correct • interesting sentences

© Harcourt

Developing Academic Language

A generalization is a broad statement about something. When people generalize, they do not usually give details or examples that support what they are saying. Generalizations help us talk about big ideas, trends, and patterns. Students will become more adept at this skill after being introduced to the words that signal a generalization.

Introduce Generalize

Show students a collection of objects that are similar in nature. For example, you might display a collection of erasers. Model how to make a generalization: *Most erasers are pink.* Write the statement on the board and draw attention to the word *most.* Ask: *Are all erasers pink? No, some are white. Some are other colors. But most of them are pink. I am making a generalization.* Explain that a generalization is a statement that says something true about many different things.

• Before **Generalize**, p. 380
• 25 minutes

Practice

Review words that are used to make generalizations, such as *most, many, usually, often, sometimes,* and *so on.* Invite students to make a sentence with each of these words. Then read the Practice paragraph in the text with students, and ask them to make a statement with the word *sometimes.* If necessary, write the following sentence on the board: *Many businesses in Alliance, Nebraska, were failing.*

Apply

On the board, draw a chart such as the one shown below. List the key ideas from the text, and then help students make a generalization based on these ideas. Gradually provide less help until students can work independently.

Key Ideas about Carhenge	Generalization
1. _____	_____
2. _____	_____
3. _____	_____
4. _____	_____

© Harcourt

Build Background

Access Prior Knowledge

Write the word *depend* on the board, and say it with the group. Say: *When you depend on someone or something, you need that person or thing.* Have students name people that they depend on, like their families, and people who depend on them, like their families, or even a pet. Then write the word *community* on the board, and say it with the group. Ask students to name or draw things in their community that they depend on. Jumpstart their ideas by suggesting that they depend on you, the teacher. Ask: *Who else do you depend on in the community?* List students' ideas on the board.

• Before **Introduce**, p. 388
• 20 minutes

Lesson Vocabulary

Display the word cards for each vocabulary word: **product, producer, entrepreneur, consumer, interdependence, wage, income.** Say a word, and exaggerate its sounds. Challenge students to study the word cards and to choose the word that you have said. You might start with an easy word, such as *wage.* When students choose the correct card, pick up the card, have students repeat the word with you, and then briefly explain what it means. For example, say: *A wage is money people get for their work.* The last two words to discuss could be *product* and *producer.* Help students recognize how the words differ. Then explain: *A product is a thing. A producer is a person. A producer makes a product.*

Additional Vocabulary Review the words or phrases in the margin in the context of the lesson, and have students make their own sentences.

Cognates As students read the lesson, you may wish to point out cognates such as: **depend/depender, interdependence/ interdependencia, product/producto, producer/productor/-ora, service/servicio.**

choose	services
fix up	share
good	trade
raise	
runs a business	

Build Fluency

Read aloud the following rhyme, and point out the words that sound alike. Return to the chant throughout the lesson to help develop vocabulary, generalization skills, and lesson content.

Producers make all kinds of things—
Products like foods, books, and rings.
Consumers buy producers' goods and games.
Their need for each other is the same.
Entrepreneurs have their own companies.
They produce things that people need.
They hire workers and give them a **wage** for each day.
It's also called an **income**—it's money they pay.
Workers need producers, producers need consumers.
That's **interdependence**—people depending on each other.

© Harcourt

Scaffolding the Content

Preview the Lesson

Preview the lesson photographs with students. Phrase questions that mimic the "What to Know" question. For example:

• During **Teach**, pp. 388–392
• 20 minutes

Page 388 Say: *Look at this picture. How do the people in this picture depend on each other?*

Page 390 Say: *Look at this picture. What is happening in these pictures?* For the smaller picture, ask: *How do the boy and the man depend on the woman? How does she depend on them?*

Page 391 Ask students to identify the people in these pictures. Point to the boy with the doctor. Ask: *How does the boy depend on the doctor? How does she depend on him?* Point to the bottom picture, and ask: *How does the family depend on the farmer? How does the farmer depend on the family?*

Modify Instruction

Tell students that in a community, everyone depends on, or needs, each other. Pass out copies of the blackline master, and point to the arrows connecting the boxes. Ask students why the arrows point in both directions. Explain that they show that people in each box depend on each other, called *interdependency*. Then begin exploring each section.

1 **People Work Together** Read the heading for the group. Ask: *How does the picture on this page show working together?* Move on to page 389. Have students recall what a producer is. Have students write *Producers make products* in the first box of their charts. Also have them write *entrepreneur*, along with *Oscar Weissenborn made pencils*. Stress that Weissenborn was a producer and an entrepreneur; pencils are the product.

2 **People Buy Things** Say: *People who buy things are consumers. Consumers buy things.* Have students write *consumers* in the second part of the chart. Discuss what the people in the pictures are buying. Ask: *What is the product?* (pencils)

3 **People Help Each Other** Have students study the blackline master. Ask: *How does this chart show that people help each other?* To prompt their ideas, ask: *How do consumers depend on producers? How do producers depend on consumers? What is this called?* (interdependency) Have students draw the images from this page on their charts. For example, the farmer and the doctor are the producers; they provide a good or a service. The boy and the family are the consumers; they buy the good or service.

4 **People Start Businesses** On the second chart, have students write *business owner* in the first box. Ask students why a business owner would need workers. (to make and sell their products) Why would workers need business owners? Have students write and draw ideas on their charts, including *wage* and *income* in the Worker box.

Extend

Have students recall how they depend on people in their community. Ask: *Which producers do you depend on? Which business owners? How do they depend on you?* Let students fill out another chart to show this interdependency in their own community.

• After **Teach**, pp. 388–392
• 15 minutes

Name _____ Date _____

Write words and pictures to show how people in a community depend on each other.

Workers and Consumers

People Work Together

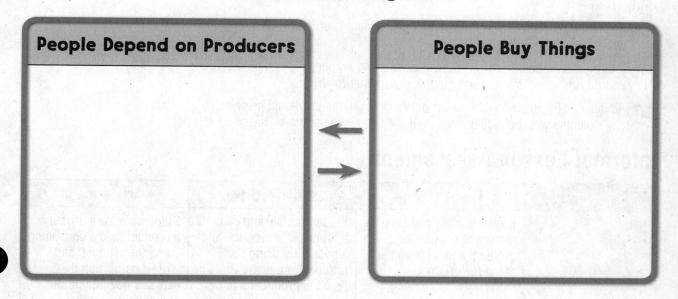

People Depend on Producers	People Buy Things

People Help Each Other

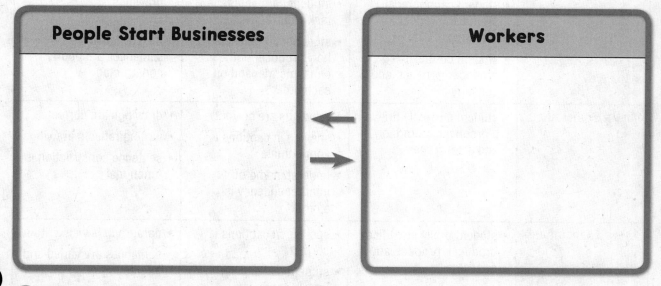

People Start Businesses	Workers

School-Home Connection Have students look around their homes for things they get from their community, such as food, library books, furniture, a local newspaper, and so on. Have students draw and label these things. Then have students tell their parents why the producers of these products need them, the consumers.

© Harcourt

Apply and Assess

Write a Help-Wanted Ad

Before the activity, reproduce and enlarge several help-wanted ads from your local newspaper. Display the ads, or pass them around the group. Explain that these ads are looking for workers. Business owners place the ads in newspapers, and workers looking for jobs reply to the ads. Brainstorm with students a business they might like to own. List ideas on the board for students to choose from. Then ask students to write a help-wanted ad to find workers.

• During **Close**, p. 392
• 45 minutes

- Beginning students can act out what a person would do at the job, along with words for you to write down.

- Intermediate students can work with partners to exchange ideas, both verbally and through pantomimes, and then work together to write.

- Advanced students should first list duties or tasks the job would involve and any skills the worker should have; then they should write the ad based on this list.

Informal Lesson Assessment

	Beginning	Intermediate	Advanced
Task	Students draw and label a picture of a producer, a product, and a consumer using the product.	Students draw and caption a producer, a product, and a consumer using the product, and orally explain how the producer and consumer depend on each other.	Students draw a producer, a product, and a consumer using the product, and write a paragraph that explains how the producer and consumer depend on each other.
Below Expectations	• student does not understand the task • student cannot recall producer, product, or consumer • student confuses producer, product, and consumer	• student cannot complete the task • student completes the task incorrectly • student cannot explain how producer and consumer depend on each other	• drawings are incorrect • writing does not reflect drawings • many words are misspelled and sentences are poorly constructed
Meets Expectations	• student correctly draws a producer, a product, and a consumer	• drawings are correct • spelling in captions is approximate • understanding of interdependency is a bit off	• drawings are correct • writing reflects drawings • sentence construction is functional
Above Expectations	• student orally identifies producer, product, and consumer	• spelling in captions is correct • student can explain interdependency	• paragraph is well written • sentences are varied and interesting

© Harcourt

Chapter

11 Build Background

Access Prior Knowledge

Have students hold up pencils, and ask: *What is a pencil made of?* Write *wood* and *graphite* on the board. Then ask: *Who made this pencil?* Write *workers* on the board. Finally, ask: *How did someone make this pencil?* Write *machine* on the board. Start a flow chart on the board. List *wood* and *graphite* in the first box, *workers* in the second box, and *machine* in the third box.

• Before **Introduce**, p. 394
• 20 minutes

Lesson Vocabulary

Point to the words *wood* and *graphite* on your flow chart. Ask students where these items come from, and agree that they come from nature. They are natural resources, or **raw materials.** Write this term in the first box. Move on to *workers.* Ask who workers are. Agree that workers are people, or **human resources.** Write this term in the second box. Finally, tell students that people buy *machines* with money. Write the word equation *money = capital* on the board. Explain that because the machines were bought with money, they are called **capital resources.** Write *capital resources* in the third box. Ask students where they might find these machines, and write *factory* on the board. Ask students what happens at the factory, and elicit such words as *make* and *produce.* Explain that another word for these terms is *manufacture.* Explain that these words tell how business works.

Additional Vocabulary Review the words or phrases in the margin in the context of the lesson, and have students make their own sentences.

Cognates As students read the lesson, you may wish to point out cognates such as: **capital/capital, human resources/recursos humanos, material/materia, machine/máquina, metal/metal, natural/natural, public/público, yogurt/yogur.**

bottle (v.)
heat (v.)
run (machine)
spring
yogurt

Build Fluency

Read aloud the following rhyme, and point out the words that sound alike. Return to the chant throughout the lesson to help develop vocabulary, generalization skills, and reinforce lesson content.

You would like to start a business! What do you need?
Listen and look closely, and you will see!
First you need **capital**—that's money. Very good!
Next are **raw materials,** like metals, rocks, and wood.
You also need people, or **human resources,** too.
And also **capital resources,** like machines and tools.
Put them all together, and you have a **factory**
To make, or **manufacture,** a product that we need.

Scaffolding the Content

Preview the Lesson

• During **Teach**, pp. 394–397
• 20 minutes

The two products described in this chapter are products students probably know. Bring in a sample of each to have on display and initiate discussion:

- Bottle of Spring Water: Hold up the spring water, and ask students to identify it. Ask students what natural resource people use to get spring water, and agree that spring water is a raw material. Direct students to the picture on page 395 to see an actual spring. Ask students to predict what else businesses might need to manufacture the spring water.

- Container of Yogurt: Hold up the yogurt, and ask students to identify it. Ask students from which raw material yogurt is made, and say: *Yogurt is made from milk. Milk is a raw material.* Let students look at the pictures on pages 396–397, and have them predict what other resources businesses might need to manufacture yogurt.

Modify Instruction

Pass out copies of the blackline master. Read the question heading, and review with students the vocabulary words they have already learned: *raw materials, human resources, capital resources.* Have students write these terms in the first column of boxes on their charts, under the "Resources" heading. Then tell students that they will look for examples of resources to write in the second column as they explore the lesson.

1. **Businesses Start with Resources** Ask students whether they think the picture on page 394 shows a natural resource or raw material, a human resource, or a capital resource. Agree that it shows a natural resource. Have students identify specific natural resources in the photograph, like water and wood (from trees). Also mention rocks and metals as raw materials. Have students write *water, wood, metal,* and *rocks* in the "Examples" column. Turn to page 395, and point to the three individual pictures. Have students choose which shows a natural resource, a human resource, and a capital resource. Have students write these examples on the chart. On a separate list, write the process of manufacturing spring water: 1) Find the spring water. 2) People collect, clean, and bottle it. 3) Machines help do these jobs, too. 4) Machines and people deliver the water. Ask students which step is done by a natural resource, a human resource, and capital resource.

2. **Working with Resources** Have students locate the human resources and the capital resources in the photograph on page 396. Mention that milk is the natural resource, or raw material, from which yogurt is made. Have students write these items in the correct boxes of the chart. Then explain that raw materials, human resources, and capital resources all come together in a building called a factory. Help students list the process of manufacturing yogurt, using the three kinds of resources.

Extend

• After **Teach**, pp. 394–397
• 15 minutes

Have students choose another item to explore, such as orange juice or bread or their school desks. Have them identify the raw materials, or natural resources, the human resources, and the capital resources needed.

© Harcourt

DIRECTIONS Write information in the chart to tell about resources that businesses use.

What Resources Do Businesses Use?

Resources	Examples

School-Home Connection Ask students to choose objects in their homes and to try to identify their raw materials. (For example, paper is made from wood.) Have students draw their objects and the raw materials, and then discuss the human and capital resources needed with family.

Apply and Assess

Make a Chart

Review with students what a flow chart is. Draw three boxes on the board—one on top, one in the middle, and one below. Connect the top box to the middle box with an arrow pointing down, and the middle box to the bottom box with an arrow pointing down. Number the boxes 1, 2, and 3. Then have students copy the flow chart and explain what is needed first, next, and last to manufacture either bottled spring water or yogurt.

• During **Close**, p. 397
• 30 minutes

- Beginning students should draw their ideas in the boxes as you prompt their ideas with key terms.
- Intermediate students can refer to the text, especially page 395, to review the resources, and then draw and label them on the chart.
- Challenge advanced students to recall the three resources on their own and then write complete sentences that tell about them.

Informal Lesson Assessment

	Beginning	Intermediate	Advanced
Task	Students point to a picture that shows a natural resource, a human resource, or a capital resource, as identified by the teacher.	Students are given a riddle and asked to identify whether the item is a natural resource, a human resource, or a capital resource.	Students write a riddle, naming a specific resource (like wood), and asking what kind of resource it is; students also provide the answer.
Below Expectations	• student does not understand the word • student points to an incorrect picture	• student does not understand the riddle • student does not name a type of resource • student names a type of resource, but it is the wrong one	• riddle does not make sense • answer is not correct in relation to the riddle • many errors in spelling and grammar
Meets Expectations	• student correctly points to a picture that shows a natural, human, or capital resource	• student correctly answers the riddle with a phrase	• riddle makes sense • answer reflects riddle • sentence construction is functional
Above Expectations	• student can identify the specific resource orally, such as *wood*	• student answers the riddle in a complete sentence	• riddle and its answer make sense • sentences are interesting • additional information and ideas included

© Harcourt

Build Background

Access Prior Knowledge

Hold up a food not produced or grown locally, such as a banana. Ask students whether it grows in their community, and agree that it does not. Ask: *How do we get _____?* Have a map on display to help students explain their answers; they might point to another country, or indicate moving from one place to another. Say: *We get things from other places. We depend on other places to get things we need.* Brainstorm with students other goods that might come from other countries.

• Before **Introduce**, p. 400
• 20 minutes

Lesson Vocabulary

Still using the same food as a prop, write the word **import** on the board. Say: *The United States imports _____. This means it buys them from other countries.* Move the prop over the map from where it is grown to the United States. On the board, write the word equation *import = into the country*. Then name a country that might **export** bananas, or sell them to other countries. Write the word *export* on the board. Say: *This country exports _____ to other countries.* On the board, write the word equation *export = out of the country*. Then write ***international trade*** on the board. Say: *Many countries import and export. We call this* international trade. *International means between countries.*

Additional Vocabulary Review the words or phrases in the margin in the context of the lesson, and have students make their own sentences.

Cognates As students read the lesson, you may wish to point out cognates such as: **interdependent/interdependiente, international/internacional, refrigerate/refrigerar.**

at least
depend on
good
interdependent
make money
make possible
newsprint
shipped

Build Fluency

Read aloud the following rhyme, and point out the words that sound alike. Return to the rhyme throughout the lesson to help develop vocabulary, generalization skills, and lesson content. These words can loosely be sung to "Twinkle, Twinkle, Little Star."

Countries trade so much today.
Why do countries like to trade?
Import goods, or things we need.
Export goods and make money.
Call it **international trade.**
Countries trade so much today.

Countries trade so much today.
What do countries like to trade?
Cars and trucks and fruit and tea,
Steel and toys and corn and beef.
What do countries like to trade?
Countries trade so much today!

© Harcourt

Scaffolding the Content

Preview the Lesson

- During **Teach**, pp. 400–403
- 20 minutes

Have students turn to page 402, and study the map. Help students read the map by pointing out the continent shapes and symbols. Then point to a continent or country, and ask students to explain what this country exports, or sends out of the country. Help students identify the symbols. Ask students where they think these goods might go. Ask: *Which country might import these goods?* Let students have fun discussing ideas.

- To reinforce the idea of trade, ask each student to draw and cut out a small picture of an item featured on the map. Have students move the picture along the map from one country to another. Ask them to say the word *export* as the item leaves a country then say *import* as the item enters a new country.

Modify Instruction

Hand out copies of the blackline master, and read the headings with the group. Explain that you would like them to discover *why* countries trade with one another. Then they will explore *what* specific goods countries trade.

1. **Depending on Each Other** Have students recall what it means to *depend on* someone. Agree that to depend on someone is to need that person. Say: *Countries depend on each other, too.* Ask students why countries might depend on each other for trade. You might recall the food prop from the "Access Prior Knowledge" activity. Lead students to understand that countries get things they need from other countries. Have students write this idea on the first line of the first box on the chart. Have students turn to page 401. Point to the transportation pictures, and have students name them as they are able. Say: *Goods must travel from place to place. Today, airplanes, trucks, ships, and barges take goods more quickly than they did long ago.* Ask students why this might be useful. After students share ideas, have them write *Trading is easier today. Goods can travel more quickly* on the second line of the graphic organizer.

2. **Where Do Goods Come From?** Invite students to answer the question posed by this section head on their own, recalling the activities they have already completed. Then explain that another reason why countries export is because they can make money. They make money by selling goods to other countries. Have students complete the last line on the chart with: *When countries export, they make money.* Then let students explore some goods that countries trade. Have them draw and label cars and trucks in the second half of their graphic organizers, as well as computers and tea. You might display newsprint paper if you have any, or a newspaper itself. Say: *The United States imports this paper from Canada.*

Extend

- After **Teach**, pp. 400–403
- 15 minutes

Assign each student a country name, or let students choose a country from the lesson. Have students write the country name on a sheet of paper, and tape it to their clothing. Then ask students to draw pictures of goods their country might trade to another country. Let students have fun "importing" and "exporting" their goods with each other.

© Harcourt

Name _____ Date _____

DIRECTIONS Write and draw information in the chart to tell about how countries trade goods with each other.

Trading with the World

Why Do Countries Trade with Each Other?

1. _____

_____

2. _____

_____

3. _____

_____

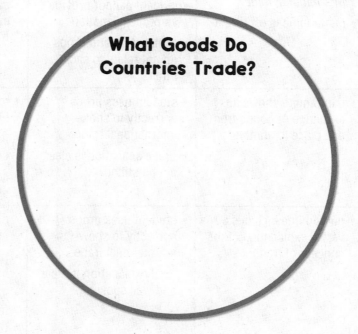

What Goods Do Countries Trade?

 School-Home Connection Have students look closely at objects at home for labels that tell where those objects were made. Have students draw the objects and label them with the country that produced and exported it. Have students share their findings with the group.

Apply and Assess

Make a Bulletin Board Display

If time allows, let students walk around the classroom to find objects made in other countries, or assign the task for homework. You might also let students draw one of the goods they read about in the lesson. Encourage students to work together to create a bulletin board display of imports.

• During **Close**, p. 403
• 30 minutes

- Beginning students can draw the item and dictate a label to you or a more proficient learner.
- Intermediate students should draw the item and write the label.
- Encourage advanced students to draw and label the object, as well as write a sentence or two that explains why we might import that object into the United States.

Informal Lesson Assessment

	Beginning	Intermediate	Advanced
Task	Students act out the meaning of international trade, either through pantomime or by using props.	Students demonstrate an understanding of international trade by using props and providing an oral explanation.	Students draw a diagram showing international trade and write a brief paragraph explaining why countries trade with each other.
Below Expectations	• student does not understand the term *international trade* • pantomime is off target	• manipulation of props is off target • student cannot provide an oral explanation • explanation and props do not relate to each other	• diagram does not show international trade • paragraph does not explain why countries trade with each other
Meets Expectations	• pantomime shows an exchange of goods from one place to another	• student uses props correctly to show international trade • oral explanation is clear, if a bit stilted	• diagram shows international trade • paragraph explains why countries trade • sentences are a bit stilted
Above Expectations	• pantomime includes a verbal explanation of the concept of trade	• student uses props correctly to show international trade • oral explanation is clear and well spoken	• diagram shows international trade • paragraph explains why countries trade • writing is engaging and interesting, with very few mistakes

© Harcourt

Build Background

Access Prior Knowledge

Hold up or point to an object that symbolizes new technology, such as a cell phone or a computer. Have students say the word for this object, and then say: *This _____ is new technology. People did not have _____ long ago.* Brainstorm with students other objects that are part of the new technology, or new inventions. Write the words for each object on the board. You might organize students' ideas in a word web, with *New Technology* in the center.

- Before **Introduce**, p. 406
- 20 minutes

Lesson Vocabulary

Say to the group: *New technology helps us. New technology helps businesses, too. These words tell about businesses and new technology.* Write the words on the board, or show students the word cards: **communication link, e-commerce, advertisement.** Review the words individually. Point to *communication,* and have students pantomime what communicate means. Explain that people use a *communication link* to send information. Point to *commerce,* and ask students what it means. Explain that people use e-commerce to buy and sell things using a computer. Cover up all but the *ad-* in *advertisement.* Ask students if they recognize this word. Show ads from a local paper, and explain that these are advertisements. They tell consumers about products a business wants to sell.

Additional Vocabulary The term *online* might confuse students. Point to a computer (or a drawing of a computer). Say: *If you are connected to the Internet, you are online.* Review other words or phrases in the margin in the context of the lesson, and have students make their own sentences.

cell phone
fax
Internet
lines
online

Cognates As students read the lesson, you may wish to point out cognates such as: **catalog/catálogo, commerce/comercio, communication/comunicación, electronic/electrónico/-a, information/información, invention/invención, technology/tecnología, telephone/teléfono.**

Build Fluency

Read aloud the following rhyme, and point out the words that sound alike. Return to the chant throughout the lesson to help develop vocabulary, generalization skills, and lesson content.

Technology changes the things we do.
Technology changes businesses, too!
Technology sends information quickly.
We can see and hear things clearly.
Technology makes **communication links**
To join computers and people who think.
Technology makes **e-commerce** work
So we can buy things, like books and shirts!
Advertisements show us things to buy.
Technology helps us! Give it a try!

© Harcourt

Scaffolding the Content

Preview the Lesson

To preview the lesson, have students think about how new technology has changed their or their parents' lives. Review the technology web you created during "Access Prior Knowledge." Then connect these ideas to the headings in the chapter. Have students find the heading *Moving Information*, and then ask them to turn to page 407. Invite students familiar with the Internet to explain the picture for classmates. Ask students how the Internet helps them. Next, ask how technology has changed the way people buy things. Agree that people can order things over the phone or over the computer. They do not need to go to the store!

• During **Teach**, pp. 406–409
• 20 minutes

Modify Instruction

Pass out two copies of the blackline master to each student. Tell students they will use the chart to show how new technology has changed businesses. Explain that in the first box, they will draw or write how the technology was first used. In the second box, they will write how the technology changed. And in the third box, they will write how the new technology changes the way people do business.

1. **Moving Information** Ask students to act out using a telephone. Have them draw or write on their charts details about people using phones. Explain that long ago, only sound could travel through a telephone line. Ask: *How is technology different today?* Today, telephone lines can send pictures and videos. People connect fax machines and computers to phone lines. Have students draw computers and fax machines in the second box. (Save the third box for later.) Have students draw a computer in the first box of the second chart. Explain that long ago, only one person could use one computer; we could not connect computers. In the second box, have students draw several connected computers. Say: *Today, computers send information to other computers!*

2. **Electronic Buying and Selling** Now have students learn how new technology changed businesses. Have students return to their phone charts. Explain how telephones and fax machines send information. Agree that people can call companies to order products. Show students mail-order catalogs, and point out the phone numbers for people to call. Return to the computer chart. Ask students how computers have changed businesses. Point to the web address on the mail-order catalogue. Explain that businesses have websites, or pages on the computer where people learn about them and their products. People can also place orders on the website. Buying things over the Internet is called e-commerce. Websites also are a form of advertisement. Have students draw these ideas in the last box of their charts.

Extend

Invite small groups of students to pretend to be a business, technology, and a customer. Give the business several lengths of yarn. Then have each technology student take a piece of yarn, and give the end to the customer. Explain that new technology connects businesses to customers, or consumers. Have the customer place an order for something, and then have the technology relay the information to the business.

• After **Teach**, pp. 406–409
• 15 minutes

© Harcourt

Name _____ Date _____

DIRECTIONS How has new technology changed businesses?
Write and draw pictures in the chart to show what you learned.

New Technology and Businesses

**How was the
technology first used?**

**How has the
technology changed?**

**How is the technology used today?
How has it changed businesses?**

 School-Home Connection Tell students to take a survey of family members, asking how many people use the
Internet for shopping or research, fax machines to send letters, and telephones for ordering and other things.
Have students share the results of the survey in class.

Apply and Assess

Write an E-mail

Write the term *e-mail* on the board. Invite students who know what it means to tell the meaning to the group. Make sure students understand that e-mail are letters sent with the computer. Say: *You can send e-mail to your friends or your family. You can send e-mail to businesses, too!* List some local businesses, and then ask students to write an e-mail letter to one of them. In their letters, have students ask the owner how changes in technology affect the business.

• During **Close**, p. 409
• 30 minutes

- Beginning students can dictate ideas to you, using simple words and phrases. Write their ideas in short sentences, modeling proper sentence construction for students.

- Intermediate students can work with partners to write a letter. Show the students a letter format to jumpstart their ideas.

- Challenge advanced students to write their letters on their own, using complete and interesting sentences.

Informal Lesson Assessment

	Beginning	Intermediate	Advanced
Task	Students draw an invention and explain how businesses use it.	Students draw an invention and write a caption that explains how businesses use it.	Students write from the point of view of a business owner, telling how technology has changed their business.
Below Expectations	• student cannot think of an invention to draw • explanation does not match drawing • explanation does not mention business	• student cannot think of an invention to draw • writing does not reflect drawing • writing does not mention business	• writing is off task • sentences do not convey ideas clearly • sentences have many mistakes in grammar and spelling
Meets Expectations	• student draws an invention • explanation matches drawing and mentions business	• student draws an invention • writing reflects drawing and mentions business • spelling is approximate	• writing is on task • sentences make sense • sentences are a bit stilted
Above Expectations	• explanation is spoken in clear sentences, with key content words	• drawing and writing are on target • sentences are well-written and spelling is correct	• writing is engaging and interesting • sentences have very few mistakes

© Harcourt

Chapter 12

Build Background

Access Prior Knowledge

Put a few dollars and coins on a table. Ask: *What are these? What are some things you use money to buy? What are some other things people buy with money? Have you ever thought about why people use money instead of something else to buy things?* Tell students that in this lesson they will learn why people use money.

• Before **Introduce**, p. 418
• 20 minutes

Lesson Vocabulary

Ask students to put pencils on their desks. Hold up a pencil of your own. Select a student. Say: *I like your pencil. Do you want to trade?* Make the trade. Then invite a few other students to trade pencils with each other. Tell students that they are bartering. Explain that to **barter** is to trade things. Tell students that when people barter they do not use money. (Be sure everyone gets back his or her own pencil.) Then ask students to draw a mint on a piece of scrap paper. Most or all will probably draw a candy. Explain that this is one meaning for **mint**. Point out that another meaning for mint is a place where money is made. Have students make up sentences using this meaning of mint.

Additional Vocabulary As you encounter multiple-meaning words in the reading, explain the common meanings. For example, explain that a *check* is a mark you put on a test next to a correct answer. It is also a form of money. Review the words or phrases in the margin in the context of the lesson, and have students make their own sentences.

account	light
bill	punch
check	stamp

Cognates As students read the lesson, you may wish to point out cognates such as: **credit/crédito.**

Build Fluency

Read aloud the following rhyme, and point out the words that sound alike. Return to the rhyme throughout the lesson to help develop vocabulary, generalizing skills, and lesson content.

I really want a catcher's mitt.
How in the world can I get it?
I can make a trade—
Barter your mitt for my lemonade.
What's another way to get it? Here's a hint:
I can pay with money from the **mint.**
Or if you can wait a minute or two,
I will write a check for you.
Or else I can give you a credit card.
That won't be very hard!

© Harcourt

Scaffolding the Content

Preview the Lesson

Read aloud the heading for each section of the lesson. Ask students to brainstorm questions they think each section might answer. Record the questions on chart paper. After completing the lesson, have students return to the list to see how many questions they can answer.

• During **Teach**, pp. 418–421
• 30 minutes

Modify Instruction

Remind students that this lesson will tell why people use money. Tell students that another way to say this is *What* causes *people to use money?* Display the Cause and Effect chart from the following page. Explain that students will use the chart to make notes about what they learn.

1 **Trading and Bartering** Ask students to give examples of some goods and services that people need. Tell them that bartering is one way to get goods. Ask: *What kind of bartering does the picture on page 418 show?* Tell students that people get services through bartering, too. Ask pairs to pretend to barter services with each other. For example: *I will help you take out the trash if you will help me fix my bike.* Point out that there can be a problem with bartering. Ask: *What would you do if you needed something but no one wanted to trade with you?* Explain that the next part of the lesson will tell about a solution to that problem. Ask students to predict the solution. Pause for students to add information to their Cause and Effect chart.

2 **Using Money to Trade** Tell students that now we use money. We trade money for things we want. It is easier to use money to buy things. Money is easy to carry. Be sure students understand that paper bills and coins are kinds of money. Then tell them that checks are something else people use to buy things. Have students find the picture of a check on page 419. People may use checks for large amounts of money, such as to pay for their house each month or to pay for electricity. Tell students that people also use credit cards to buy things. Have them find a picture of a credit card on the page. Explain that when people want to buy something, they show their credit cards. They promise to pay for the thing later. Call attention to the graphic on page 420. Tell students that people have used money for thousands of years. In the past, people used other things, such as beads and shells. Ask students to fill in what they learned on the Cause and Effect chart.

3 **United States Money** Philadelphia was the first place to make money in the United States. That happened in 1792. Coins are made in a mint from metal strips. The strips are put into a machine. Round shapes are cut out of the strips. Pictures and words are put on both sides of the shapes. Have students draw the three steps you described.

Extend

Have small groups use picture books about different countries to find out about money in those cultures. Also, encourage students to use their own prior knowledge about kinds of money from living in, or visiting other places. Have each group show pictures of money from the picture books, and tell what those kinds of money are called.

• After **Teach**, pp. 418–421
• 25 minutes

© Harcourt

Why Do People Use Money?

Cause People have things that other people need.	→	**Effect** _____ _____
Cause No one wants to barter.	→	**Effect** _____ _____
Cause Someone wants to make a large payment.	→	**Effect** _____ _____
Cause Someone wants to buy something now and pay later.	→	**Effect** _____ _____
Cause People did not have coins and paper money long ago.	→	**Effect** _____ _____

School-Home Connection Have students take this page home to share with their families. They can use the information on the chart to tell what kinds of money we use and why we use them.

Apply and Assess

Make a Coin Display

• During **Close**, p. 421
• 20 minutes

Show students a penny, nickel, dime, and quarter. Name each coin, and have students repeat its name after you. Then hold up each coin again, and tell its value. Say: *A penny is one cent; a nickel is five cents; a dime is ten cents; a quarter is twenty-five cents.* Then randomly hold up the coins, and have students name each coin, and tell its value. Ask students to use this information to make their displays.

- Put the names of the coins and their values on the board. Invite beginning language learners to copy this information to make their displays.

- Show intermediate learners how to write the value of coins in two forms: *one cent* and *1¢*. Ask them to include both on their displays.

- Challenge advanced learners to write a card to accompany the display. Tell them to give the display a title, and explain it on the card.

Informal Lesson Assessment

	Beginning	Intermediate	Advanced
Task	Students draw labeled pictures showing the kinds of money people use and why they use it.	Students use sentences to answer the following questions: *How do people get goods and services? Why do people use money?*	Students write a short report telling ways people buy things and why they use money.
Below Expectations	• unable to create pictures • creates pictures but cannot verbalize about them	• unable to respond • responds with irrelevant or incorrect information	• unable to respond • responds with ideas that are not in paragraph form
Meets Expectations	• creates pictures of money, checks, and credit cards • shows someone making a purchase	• gives at least one way people get goods and services • provides at least one reason people use money	• mentions the use of barter and money • gives general information about when people use cash, checks, and credit cards
Above Expectations	• illustrates money, checks, and credit cards • shows people purchasing both goods and services	• discusses both bartering and using money • tells why people use cash, checks, and credit cards	• explains barter and use of money, giving examples • describes and explains use of cash, checks, and credit cards

© Harcourt

Build Background

Access Prior Knowledge

With students, plan an imaginary lemonade stand. Discuss materials needed to start and run it. Ask students how much people would pay for their product. Tell students they will learn about how businesses work in this lesson.

- Before **Introduce**, p. 422
- 30 minutes

Lesson Vocabulary

Point out that the class could start a business because the United States has a **free market.** This means that people can sell any product or service that our laws allow. Tell students that the money they make from selling lemonade would be the **profit.** Profit is the money left after they pay for lemons and sugar. Introduce the term **demand.** Explain that demand is the number of people who want to buy a product. Ask: *On a very hot day, is the* demand *for lemonade high or low?* Next, tell students that **supply** means how much of the product there is to sell. Ask: *If someone accidentally spills a cup of our lemonade, does the* supply *go up or down?* Ask students to imagine that a lot of people came to the stand. There was not enough lemonade for everyone. Tell them that **scarcity** describes not having enough for everyone. Finally, ask students to imagine that another class started a lemonade stand. Tell students that the other class would be their **competition.** They would be trying to sell lemonade to the same people! Ask: *What other businesses might be in* competition *with us on a hot day?*

Additional Vocabulary Review the words in the margin in the context of the lesson, and have students make their own sentences.

Cognates As students read the lesson, you may wish to point out cognates such as: **demand/demanda.**

contest
draw
low
raised
run

Build Fluency

Read aloud the following rhyme, and point out the words that sound alike. Return to the rhyme throughout the lesson to help develop vocabulary, generalizing skills, and lesson content.

A **free market** is all about **demand** and **supply.**
If demand is up and supplies go down
Profits go high as the sky.

When there is **scarcity**
There's not enough of what we need.
That causes prices to go up, you see.

But it all works out in the end.
Competition helps the market run as it should.
Businesses have a contest about
Who can sell the most services and goods.

© Harcourt

Scaffolding the Content

Preview the Lesson

Guide students in a picture walk of the lesson. Talk about each photo with them, encouraging students to use some of the vocabulary words in the discussion. Tell students they will learn how a free market works.

• During **Teach**, pp. 422–425
• 30 minutes

Modify Instruction

Distribute copies of the blackline master page. Tell students that the lesson will help them decide how to label parts of the picture.

1 **A Free Market Economy** Tell students that people can start any kind of business they wish in the United States. Tell students that people make products or do services to earn money, or make a profit. Have students tell what products or services businesses in the ads provide. Explain that to earn money, businesses must spend money. Use the example of a lawn-mowing business. The owners have to buy mowers and gas. Tell students that a person with a lawn-mowing business adds up the money people pay for mowing. Then the owner subtracts how much it costs to buy the mower, gas, and other things he or she needs. The money that is left is the profit. Ask students what kinds of things the businesses they have identified might need to spend money on.

2 **Competition in a Free Market** Have students find examples of competing businesses in the ads. For example, they might identify all the grocery stores. Tell students that competition can affect prices. Point out ads for the same item, such as milk, at two grocery stores. Have students compare prices. Ask: *Are the prices almost the same? What would happen if one store made its price much lower? What would the other store probably have to do?* Explain that stores cannot make their prices too low. If they do, they will not make a profit.

3 **Supply and Demand** When people want something, we say there is a demand for that thing. If people want a lot of something, businesses make and sell a lot of it. They make a large supply of it. Direct attention to the chart on page 424, and explain it. Ask questions such as: *Would prices go up or down if there was a lot of an item?*

4 **Scarcity of Products** Explain that sometimes lots of people want an item but there is not enough for everyone. For example, people need a lot of wheat. Wheat is used to make bread, cereal, cookies, and many other things. If there is not much rain, farmers cannot grow enough wheat for all the people who want it. Then we have a scarcity of wheat. Wheat costs more to buy.

Have students revisit the headings and pictures to help them recall the ideas from the lesson. Then ask them to use what they learned to label the blackline master. Ask students to explain their answers once they have finished.

Extend

As a class, have students decide on a particular type of business, such as a car wash. Have small groups create a name for their car wash. Ask them to talk about how they would make a profit. Have them decide how they will compete with the other groups' car washing businesses. Provide time for groups to share their ideas with each other.

• After **Teach**, pp. 422–425
• 25 minutes

© Harcourt

Name _____ Date _____

| competition | demand | free market | profit | supply |

This shows an example of a _____ _____.

School-Home Connection Have students take this page home to share with their families. They can use the picture to explain how a free market works.

Unit 6, Chapter 12, Lesson 2

Success for English Learners ■ **173**

© Harcourt

Apply and Assess

Write a Paragraph

• During **Close**, p. 425
• 30 minutes

Have students revisit the local newspaper they used during the lesson. Ask each to cut out an ad for a store or service business. Have students identify the good or service their selected business provides. Also, have students look back at the chart on page 424. Have them talk about the chart, using specific details related to their chosen business. For example, a student might say: *If there is a high demand for toys, my business could sell toys for more money.* Tell students to use ideas from their discussion to complete the assignment.

- Help beginning learners create a group chart like the one on page 424 for their selected business. Then have them dictate sentences to you about the information on the chart.

- Provide a paragraph frame for intermediate learners to use. For example:

  More people want _____. The cost _____. Not many people want _____. The cost _____. There are a lot of _____. The cost _____. There are not many _____. The cost _____.

- Ask advanced learners to begin their paragraphs with a topic sentence that gives the main idea of what they will discuss. Encourage them to use cause-effect words, such as *so* and *because*.

Informal Lesson Assessment

	Beginning	Intermediate	Advanced
Task	Students draw a picture similar to the one on the blackline master for a different business and label the parts.	Students make up sentences telling about a free-market economy. Display the vocabulary words, and ask students to use as many as possible.	Students write a paragraph explaining how a free-market economy works.
Below Expectations	• unable to create a relevant picture • creates a picture but is unable to label or discuss it	• unable to write about a free-market economy • writes about a free-market economy but does not use any vocabulary words	• unable to respond • responds with sentences that are not organized into a paragraph
Meets Expectations	• creates a labeled picture • uses words and phrases to tell about the picture	• writes about a free-market economy • uses at least three vocabulary words	• writes basic facts about a free-market economy • uses paragraph form
Above Expectations	• creates a labeled picture • uses simple sentences to tell what it shows	• writes about a free-market economy • uses all the vocabulary words	• writes an organized paragraph explaining a free-market economy • gives an overview and provides examples

© Harcourt

Build Background

Access Prior Knowledge

Ask students what they have bought recently. Then ask how they got the money to buy it (allowance, gift, doing extra chores, selling something they own). Record ideas on a web titled *Ways to Get Money.* Tell students they will learn how families get money and what they do with it.

• Before **Introduce**, p. 426
• 30 minutes

Lesson Vocabulary

Point out the illustration on page 430. Say that it shows a **budget.** Explain that a budget is a plan for spending and saving money. It shows how much money a person gets. It also shows what he or she does with the money. Have students point to the part that shows money someone gets. Ask them to identify items someone uses money for. Next, display a piggy bank or a homemade bank. Place a few coins in it. Say that some of the money in a budget is used for **savings.** Explain that savings is made up of money people do not spend. Let students place pennies in the bank, and use the vocabulary word to tell what they are doing. Point out that we can save a little money at home. It is a good idea, however, to put or **deposit,** most of our savings in a bank. Have students look at the picture of the bank on page 429. Tell students that banks pay people to keep money there. The money a bank pays is called **interest.** Write a savings amount on the board. Write an amount for interest under it. Have students add the numbers to show how money increases in a bank.

Additional Vocabulary Remind students that many words have more than one meaning. For example, soccer players in the class might be familiar with the word *goal.* However, in the lesson, *goal* refers to something you want to do in the future. Review the terms in the margin in the context of the lesson, and have students make their own sentences.

account	part
follow (a budget)	reach
goal	shelter
manage	take classes

Cognates As students read the lesson, you may wish to point out cognates such as: **deposit/depósito, interest/interés, bank/banco.**

Build Fluency

Read aloud the following rhyme, and point out the words that sound alike. Return to the rhyme throughout the lesson to help develop vocabulary, generalizing skills, and lesson content.

A **budget** helps families plan how to use their money.
Here are the steps to follow: one, two, three.

First, families must figure out their total income.
What each person earns is added to get the sum.

Then they decide how much they can spend
To get things for themselves and for their friends.

Finally, they **deposit** the rest in their **savings** banks,
Which pay them **interest** to say, "Thanks!"

© Harcourt

Scaffolding the Content

Preview the Lesson

Read each lesson heading to students. Let them tell anything they already know about each topic, and list it on the board. Encourage a few questions about each topic, and list them on the board. Tell students that they will learn more about the topics of earning, spending, and saving in the lesson. When the lesson is completed, have students use the chart they completed during the lesson to summarize what they learn.

• During **Teach**, pp. 426–431
• 30 minutes

Modify Instruction

Distribute copies of the blackline master page. Explain that students will use it to take notes about what they learn from the lesson.

1 **A Family Earns Income** Say: *Meet the Wright family.* Point to the boy on page 426. *James is the son.* Point to the woman and man on page 427. *Bonnie is the mother. Ed is the father.* Tell students that they will learn about earning, spending, and saving by finding out what this family does with their money. Explain that families earn money or income in many ways. James gets paid to clean up his neighbors' yards. Bonnie gets paid to take photos of special events. Ed got paid to make car parts. Then he went to school to learn something new. Now he gets paid to be a manager. He helps workers in a factory. Ask: *What other ways do people earn money?* Have students add ideas to their charts.

2 **A Family Spends and Saves** Explain that the Wrights decide how to spend the money they make. They spend money for things they need, such as food, clothes, and their house. They also buy things they want, like karate lessons, movie tickets, and CDs. This family uses some of their money to help others and also saves some of their money. Ask: *What are other things people use money for? Which are things they need? Which are things they want but do not need?* Tell students to add ideas to the second column of their chart.

3 **Saving Money** Point out that the Wrights do not spend all their money. They save some money in a bank. The bank gives them money called interest so their money increases, or grows, in the bank. Sometimes people borrow money from banks, too. If the Wrights wanted to buy a new car, they might borrow money from their bank. The bank would make them pay for the right to borrow the money. The extra money they would pay is also called interest. Ask: *What are other reasons people borrow money?* Tell students to put ideas from this part of the lesson on their charts.

4 **A Family Makes a Budget** Tell students that the Wrights make a plan for their money. They list all the money they earn. They list all the money they spend. This plan, or budget, helps them know where their money goes. It also helps them do things they want to do. Ask: *What problems could the Wrights have if they did not have a budget?* Have students add ideas from this section to the last column of their charts.

Extend

Have groups of four work together. One student will role-play being a bank worker. The others will role-play being members of a family. Tell the family to talk to the bank worker about their income, spending, and savings. Encourage groups to use the lesson vocabulary.

• After **Teach**, pp. 426–431
• 15 minutes

© Harcourt

Name _____ Date _____

Earning	Spending	Saving	Budgets
What I Learned	What I Learned	What I Learned	What I Learned
_____	_____	_____	_____
_____	_____	_____	_____
_____	_____	_____	_____
_____	_____	_____	_____
_____	_____	_____	_____
_____	_____	_____	_____
_____	_____	_____	_____
_____	_____	_____	_____
_____	_____	_____	_____
_____	_____	_____	_____
_____	_____	_____	_____
_____	_____	_____	_____
_____	_____	_____	_____
_____	_____	_____	_____
_____	_____	_____	_____
_____	_____	_____	_____
_____	_____	_____	_____
_____	_____	_____	_____
_____	_____	_____	_____

School-Home Connection Have students take this page home to share with their families. They can use the
information on the chart to tell what they learned about earning, spending, saving, and budgeting money.

Apply and Assess

Make a Budget

Have students brainstorm financial goals that someone their age might have, such as saving to buy a new bike. List goals on the board. Then help students brainstorm ways to earn money, such as raking leaves or taking care of pets. Keep the two lists and the web on display as students work on their budgets. Help them make realistic estimates of how much money they could earn with each task and how much it will take to reach their financial goals.

• During **Close**, p. 431
• 20 minutes

- Allow beginning learners to use labeled drawings on their budgets.
- Ask intermediate learners to present their budget in words and phrases.
- Encourage advanced learners to use dictionaries to check the spellings of words on their budgets.

Informal Lesson Assessment

	Beginning	Intermediate	Advanced
Task	Students create a comic strip showing how a family earns, spends, and saves money.	Students create a comic strip with dialogue, showing how a family earns, spends, and saves money.	Students write two or three paragraphs or a very short story about a family earning, spending, and saving money for a goal.
Below Expectations	• unable to create a comic strip • creates a comic strip, but no accurate information presented	• unable to create a comic strip • creates a comic strip but does not address the lesson content	• unable to produce paragraphs or a story • produces a story but does not address the prompt
Meets Expectations	• completes the comic strip with pictures and words • incorporates some of the key information from the lesson	• creates a comic strip about earning, spending, and saving • uses illustrations and character dialogue to address several key ideas from the lesson	• writes paragraphs or a story that generally addresses the prompt • includes several concepts from the lesson
Above Expectations	• completes the comic strip with words and possibly phrases • incorporates all the key information from the lesson	• draws and writes creatively to address the topic • includes most of the key concepts from the lesson	• writes detailed paragraphs or a creative, detailed story • includes most or all of the key concepts from the lesson

Build Background

Access Prior Knowledge

Invite students to share what they know about businesses in other countries they have lived in or visited. Ask: *What were some goods people sold? What were some services they sold? In what ways were those businesses like businesses in the United States? How were they different?* Point out that people in countries all over the world have businesses. Tell students that this lesson will tell about some businesses around the world.

• Before **Introduce**, p. 436
• 25 minutes

Lesson Vocabulary

Remove a pile of books from your classroom bookshelves. Select several students, and say: *I would like you to work together. I would like you to cooperate to put the books back on the shelves.* Have the class watch as the group performs the task. Then talk with students about what it means to cooperate. Write the word *cooperate* on the board. Write **cooperative** beside it. Ask students to tell what is the same about the two words. Tell students that a cooperative is a group of people who own a business together. They work together, or cooperate, to make the business work. Ask students to think of examples of ways people might work together in a cooperative.

Additional Vocabulary As you encounter in the reading the words in the margin, explain the common meanings, and review their meanings in the context of the lesson. For example, explain that to *keep offices* means to have offices. Help students use context to figure out the meanings and make their own sentences.

feed
keep offices
raise
ship

Cognates As students read the lesson, you may wish to point out cognates such as: **cooperative/cooperativa, depend/depender, local/local.**

Build Fluency

Read aloud the following rhyme, and point out the words that sound alike. Return to the rhyme throughout the lesson to help develop vocabulary, generalizing skills, and lesson content.

There are businesses in every country you can name.
But they are not at all the same!

Some are big computer companies in cities like Tokyo.
Other businesses are small farming **cooperatives,** you know.

Some businesses keep the goods they make from day to day.
Others export their goods to countries far away.

© Harcourt

Scaffolding the Content

Preview the Lesson

Ask students to look at the lesson photos. Explain that they all show businesses in other countries. Discuss with students how these businesses are similar to and different from businesses in their community. Tell students they will learn about how these businesses make money.

• During **Teach**, pp. 436–439
• 30 minutes

Modify Instruction

Hand out copies of the Main Idea Table from the next page, and read aloud the main idea. Tell students they will look for ideas that support the main idea as they work on the lesson.

1 **A Business District** Tell students that all countries have businesses. Families depend on those businesses for goods and services. Have students look at the picture on page 436. Explain that it shows businesses in the city of Tokyo in Japan. Locate Tokyo on a world map. Tell students that many Japanese businesses have their main offices in Tokyo. Businesses from some other countries also have their main offices in Tokyo.

2 **Businesses Depend on One Another** Explain that businesses work together. For example, a business in Tokyo makes computers. That business depends on other businesses that make parts for computers. It also depends on transportation companies to take the computers to stores. The computer business depends on stores to sell their computers. Some of the computers made in Tokyo are sold to people in Japan. Some of them are sold to people in other countries. Pause to let students write some ideas they have learned so far on the Main Idea Table.

3 **A Community Cooperative** Call attention to the photos on page 438. Tell students they will learn about a very different kind of business. It is not in a big city like Tokyo. It is in a small village in the country of Mozambique. Locate the country on a map. The business people there do not make computers. They are farmers who grow sunflowers. They feed the sunflowers to chickens to help the chickens grow. Then they sell the chickens to make money. The farmers have a cooperative. They own the farm together. They all help each other with the business. They all share the money they earn. Ask students to add more details to the Main Idea Table. Tell them they can add more legs to the table, if needed.

Extend

Have small groups imagine that they want to start a cooperative business. First, ask them to decide what their business will sell. Then ask them to role-play having a meeting to decide how to start and run their business. Provide time for groups to summarize for the class what they discussed.

• After **Teach**, pp. 436–439
• 20 minutes

© Harcourt

Name _____ Date _____

Listen as your teacher reads the main idea. Then listen as he/she summarizes the lesson. Write details in the legs of the table that support the main idea.

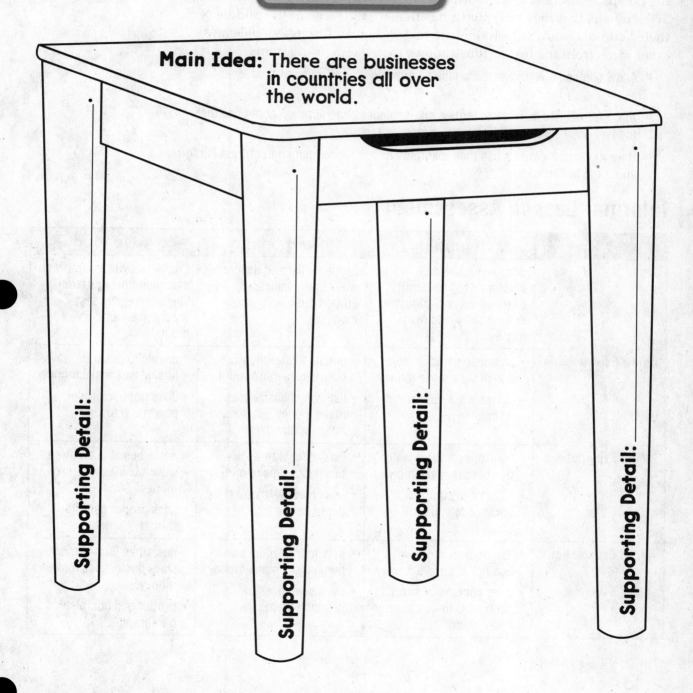

Main Idea Table

Main Idea: There are businesses in countries all over the world.

Supporting Detail:

Supporting Detail:

Supporting Detail:

Supporting Detail:

© Harcourt

 School-Home Connection Have students take this page home to share with their families. They can use the information on the Main Idea Table to summarize the most important ideas in the lesson.

Apply and Assess

Make a Diagram

First, ask students to identify the two businesses used as the main examples in this lesson. Encourage them to tell what they remember about each business. List the details they recall under the headings *Tokyo Computer Business* and *Mozambique Farming Cooperative*. After listing the details, ask students to notice anything that is the same in both lists. Tell students that they will put things that are the same in the middle of their Venn diagram. Ask students to use ideas they discussed, plus any other ideas from the text or illustrations, to make their diagrams.

• During **Close**, p. 439
• 25 minutes

- Allow beginning learners to use labeled drawings for as many of their ideas as they wish.

- Ask intermediate learners to write a one-sentence generalization about whether the two businesses are more alike or more different.

- Have advanced learners use their diagrams to write a comparison/contrast paragraph about the businesses.

Informal Lesson Assessment

	Beginning	**Intermediate**	**Advanced**
Task	Students make an illustrated list to identify different ways businesses around the world make money.	Students list and describe ways that businesses around the world make money.	Students write a paragraph describing how different kinds of businesses around the world make money.
Below Expectations	• unable to identify ways businesses make money • makes a list but cannot discuss it	• unable to identify ways businesses make money • lists ways businesses make money but does not describe them	• unable to describe ways businesses make money • does not use proper paragraph format
Meets Expectations	• lists at least three ways businesses make money • uses words and/or phrases to verbalize about the list	• lists at least three ways businesses make money • uses phrases to describe items on the list	• describes at least three ways businesses make money • uses proper paragraph format
Above Expectations	• lists four or more ways businesses make money • uses phrases or short sentences to verbalize about them	• lists four or more ways businesses make money • uses sentences to describe them	• describes four or more ways businesses make money • produces a complete paragraph

© Harcourt

Answer Key

Chapter 1

Lesson 1 What Is a Community?, p. 4

People = Many People, One Community:
Children should draw self-portraits inside this box, along with portraits of other people in their community, such as family members, their teachers, their classmates, a shop owner they might know, their mail carrier, a librarian, and so on, labeling them as they are able.

Businesses = Depending on One Another:
Children should draw and label businesses in their community, such as specific shops, stores, a mall, and restaurants. Make sure children do not draw a public service, like a library or a post office.

Play and Learn = Coming Together: Children should draw and label community places where people have fun, such as a community park, a movie theater, an arcade, a sports field, or a playground.

Following Rules and Laws: Review students' answers for an understanding of the concept. Students might draw a traffic light or a stop sign, or "open" and "closed" signs at a park, or draw a list of rules posted in your classroom.

Lesson 2 Communities Are Different, p. 8

Some Communities: drawings will vary, but might include flat land, hills, mountains, rain, snow

All communities: geography, climate, landforms

Other communities: drawings will vary, but might include flat land, hills, mountains, rain, snow and other features not mentioned previously

Lesson 3 Communities Are Connected, p. 12

Nation: United States
Community 1: Saint Louis, MO
Community 2: Bogor
Communication: telephone, letters, e-mail, conversation, fax, television, radio
Community 3: will vary
Community 4: will vary
Nations: will vary

Lesson 4 Discover Your Community, p. 16

Chart 1—Interview Someone in Your Community:

1. Find someone to ask.
2. Write the questions.
3. Ask the questions.

Chart 2—Write to or Visit Special Places:

1. Find a place to visit.
2. Decide what you need.
3. Ask for what you need.

Chapter 2

Lesson 1 Urban Communities, p. 20

Many people: all cities; **Tall buildings:** all cities; **Many businesses:** all cities; **A harbor**: Baltimore, New York City, Los Angeles; **Transportation:** all cities

Lesson 2 Suburban Communities, p. 24

Maplewood: houses, tree-lined streets, small stores, shopping centers, parks, movie theaters, supermarkets, schools

Connections: roads, cars, trains, subways

New York City: theaters, museums, cultural attractions, sports arenas

Lesson 3 Rural Communities, p. 28

Searcy: county fair, local community center

Urban and Suburban Connections: roads, cars, trains, subways

Other Rural Communties: universities and colleges, historic sites, outdoor activities

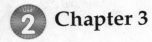 **Chapter 3**

Lesson 1 Our Location, p. 33

Planet: Earth; **Hemisphere:** Northern; **Continent:** North America; **Country:** United States; **State/Region:** will vary; **Community:** will vary

Lesson 2 Our Country's Geography, p. 37

Physical Features: land features, bodies of water, climate and weather, physical processes

Lesson 3 Our Country's Regions, p. 41

Our Country's Regions: Student maps should show correct location of the Northeast, Southeast, Middle West, West, and Southwest.

Lesson 4 Natural Resources, p. 45

Natural Resources: trees, land, water, minerals; drawing of each; **Renewable Resources:** trees, animals; **Non-Renewable Resources:** minerals **Living Resources:** trees, animals; **Non-Living Resources:** water, metals, soil, minerals

 Chapter 4

Lesson 1 People and the Environment, p. 49

Where people live: mountains, beaches, cities, deserts; **How people live:** In the desert, people might not have lawns. In Africa, the Masai wear loose clothing because it is so hot. Where it is cold, people drive snowmobiles.

People and natural disasters: Students should draw and label a tornado; cars covered with snow (snow); dry land (drought); a street covered with water (flood).

Lesson 2 How People Modify the Environment, p. 53

Transportation: drawing of canal, with label; drawing of tunnel, with label

Farming and Mining: drawing of terrace farming, with label; drawing of irrigation, with label; mine and minerals, with labels

Water and Electricity: drawing of dam and reservoir, with labels; drawing of water and dam, with labels; drawing of wind and wind turbines, with labels

Lesson 3 Caring for Our Environment, p. 57

Controlling Pollution: drawing of ways reduce smoke from factories and exhaust from cars, with label

Causes of Pollution: drawing of trash, with label; drawing of factories and smoke, with label; drawing of cars and exhaust, with label

Reducing Pollution: drawing of car with no exhaust, with the label "hybrid car"

Conserving Our Resources: drawing of person turning off water faucet or using both sides of a sheet of paper

Reusing Resources: drawing of recycling bins, with labels such as "paper, cans, bottles" on bins, and the label "recycling" for the entire drawing; student might also draw an item that he or she reuses, with the label "reuse"

A Plan for the Future: Answers will vary, but student's ideas should reflect a plan to help care for the environment, such as cleaning a neighborhood park, setting up a recycling center at school, and so on.

Chapter 5

Lesson 1 Communities Through Time, p. 62

Same:

There were some tall buildings; people went to work in big buildings; most people worked in the city and lived outside the city.

Different:

There are many more tall building now; how people went to work has changed: now most people drive cars or use public transportation, but in those times, people walked or rode horses; the kind of work people do has changed; the tools people use for work has changed: work was more manual, today we have computers; the materials used to make building has changed, less wood, more concrete and metals; more people live and work in the city now.

Lesson 2 People Change Communities, p. 66

What?	Why?	Who?
new roads, canals, railroads	to connect communities	people who live there
locomotive	to get places faster and easier	George Stephenson
more buildings	for more places to live and work	people who live in the community
steel and iron buildings	so people could make taller buildings	William Jenney
elevators	so people could live and work in tall buildings	Elisha Otis
suffrage for women	so they would have the same rights as men	Susan B. Anthony, Elizabeth Cady Stanton
freedom	so India could make its own laws	Mohandas Gandhi
civil rights	so everyone was treated fairly	Dr. Martin Luther King, Jr.

Lesson 3 Inventions in Communities, p. 70

Communication: the Pony Express, telegraph, telephone; **Transportation:** canals, railroads, automobiles, lower-cost automobiles, airplanes; **Home:** electric light bulbs, televisions, radios, stoves, ovens, dishwashers, refrigerators

Lesson 4 Communities in Ancient Times, p. 74

Mesopotamia: first cities, wheeled carts, writing; **Egypt:** pyramids, use of wheels, pulleys, ramps to move heavy stones; **China:** paper, printing, fireworks; **Greece:** first democracy, artists, builders, writers; **Rome:** first republic, rich cities; **Mali:** trading center

 Chapter 6

Lesson 1 Our First Communities, p. 78

Who? Native Americans; **Where?** Every part of the United States, along rivers east of the Mississippi, on farms in the Southeast, near rivers and oceans in the Northwest; **When?** Long ago; **What?** Forests, rivers, clay, buffalo, corn, beans, squash; **How?** In many ways, in wood shelters, in clay brick homes, in longhouses, teepees, gathering food, hunting animals, farming; **My question:** Answers will vary.

Lesson 2 Building Communities, p. 82

1492: Columbus reaches the Americas; **1565:** St. Augustine is started; **1607:** English explorers start Jamestown; **1612:** settlers start growing tobacco; **1619:** Africans are forced to be slaves; **1620:** English settlers start Plymouth; **1763:** St. Louis is started.

Lesson 3 Fighting for Our Freedoms, p. 86

Sample answers: **Tea Party in Boston Harbor!** The colonists were very mad about taxes. They threw English tea in the water; **War!** The colonists want to be free. The English do not want them to be free. They are fighting a war; **Colonists Declare Independence!** Leaders wrote a paper. It said they wanted to start their own country; **War Ends!** The American soldiers were brave. They won the war. We have our own country. It is the United States. Now, we need to make laws.

Lesson 4 Growth and Change, p. 90

Jefferson asked Lewis and Clark to explore. They wrote about what they saw, and this made people want to see it too; some people could not get jobs or land in the East, so they traveled West; the North and South had different ideas about slavery and other things, so they fought; railroads and new roads were built and this made it easier for people to travel; immigrants came to the United States. Hawaii and Alaska became states. These things added new people to our country.

Chapter 7

Lesson 1 Rights of Citizens, p. 95

First graphic organizer, text for box: Bill of Rights; Constitution. Text for circles: freedom of speech; freedom of assembly; freedom of the press; freedom of religion
Second graphic organizer, text for box: Citizens Make Choices; citizens = people; text for circles: election; ballot; majority rule = the most; minority rights = the least

Lesson 2 Duties of Citizens, p. 99

Our Responsibilities:
1. obey laws
2. pay taxes
3. serve on a jury
Serving Your Community:
1. for the common good
2. volunteer

Lesson 3 Being a Good Citizen, p. 103

What Is a Good Citizen? follows laws; speaks out against things that are unfair; does their best; is responsible; is respectful; helps others; **Jimmy Carter:** works for peace, volunteers; **Rosa Parks:** spoke out against unfair laws, caused change; **Dolores Huerta:** helped others; **Everyday Heroes:** firefighters, police officers, teachers, volunteers: help others, follow laws, are responsible, do their best.

Chapter 8

Lesson 1 Structure of Government, p. 107

Branches of Government: legislative, executive, judicial; Levels of Government: local, state, national or federal

Lesson 2 Local Governments, p. 111

Middle Section: city and town government; county government; community services
Bottom Section: mayor; mayor-council/council-management; county board/county seat/county courts/laws/offices/judges; police/schools/sports/parks/trash/public works

Lesson 3 State and National Governments, p. 115

State Governments: Executive Branch: governor; suggests laws; carries out laws. Legislative Branch: makes laws; lawmakers; capitol building. Judicial Branch: U.S. Supreme Court; courts and judges. Services: highways, state parks; provide goods

National Government:
Executive Branch: president; leads military; suggests laws; Washington, D.C.; White House. Legislative Branch: Congress; House of Representatives; Senate; new laws. Judicial: Supreme Court; nine judges; laws are constitutional; appointed by President. Services: the mail; national parks; provide goods

Lesson 4 Symbols of Our Nation, p. 119

Top Circle: American flag; Side Circles: bald eagle, Liberty Bell; Bottom Circle (Monuments and Memorials): Washington Monument, Lincoln Memorial, National World War II Memorial, Korean War Veterans Memorial, Franklin Delano Roosevelt Memorial, Vietnam Veterans Memorial; Bottom Circle (Words of Patriotism): Anthem = "The Star-Spangled Banner." Pledge = the Pledge of Allegiance

Lesson 5 Governments of the World, p. 123

Mexico—<u>Leader:</u> president <u>Branches:</u> executive, legislative, judicial

Canada—<u>Leader:</u> prime minister (executive branch) <u>Branches:</u> legislative branch = Parliament; executive branch = Cabinet of Ministers

Bhutan—<u>Leader:</u> king or monarch: King Jigme Singye Wangchuck; royal family <u>Branches:</u> constitutional monarchy; monarch and government elected by people; legislative branch = National Assembly; executive branch = Council of Ministers

 Chapter 9

Lesson 1 Moving to New Places, p. 128

Chart 1—**Where Did They Come From?** Europe, Africa, South America, Australia, Asia; **Where Did They Move?** the United States; **Why Did They Move?** for new opportunities, freedoms, a better education, jobs, and to escape dangers in their country

Chart 2—**Where Did They Come From?** African Americans came from rural places in the South; **Where Did They Move?** cities in the Northeast, Midwest, and West; **Why Did They Move?** to find new opportunities, more freedoms, an education, jobs, and to escape dangers where they lived

Lesson 2 Sharing Cultures, p. 132

Chart 1—**City:** Washington, D.C. **Ethnic Groups:** Chinese, Latin American, Caribbean, African, Asian; **How They Share Their Cultures:** restaurants and shops

Chart 2—**City:** Cleveland, Ohio **Ethnic Groups:** African Americans, Italian, Czech, Irish, Polish; **How They Share Their Cultures:** Cleveland Cultural Gardens, neighborhood events, African American Museum

Chart 3—**City:** Chamblee, Georgia **Ethnic Groups:** Mexican, Vietnamese, Greek, Thai, Chinese; **How They Share Their Cultures:** restaurants, bookstores, music stores

Lesson 3 Our American Heritage, p. 136

What Makes Up Our American Heritage? culture, customs, traditions, and beliefs <u>American Landmarks</u>—Statue of Liberty, Mount Rushmore <u>What it Honors</u>—Freedom, our presidents <u>Holidays</u>—Veteran's Day, Fourth of July, President's Day <u>Who it Honors</u>—U.S. veterans, our country's independence, our presidents

 Chapter 10

Lesson 1 Expressions of Culture, p. 140

Written and Oral Language—<u>Center Circle:</u> Written and Oral Language, Literature <u>Outer Circles:</u> fable/drawing of animal; myth/ drawing of nature; folktale/drawing of person; legend/drawing of person;

The Arts—<u>Center Circle:</u> The Arts <u>Outer Circles:</u> mural/drawing of mural; folk song/drawing of someone singing; dance/ drawing of someone dancing; buildings/drawing of pyramid;

Religions—<u>Center Circle:</u> Religions, Worship <u>Outer Circles:</u> Christians, churches; Muslims, mosque or masjid; Jewish people, synagogue or temple; Buddhists and Hindus, temples

Lesson 2 Holidays and Traditions, p. 144

Cultural Holidays—<u>Section 1:</u> Saint Patrick's Day; Irish culture; colors of green, orange, and white; <u>Section 2:</u> Cinco de Mayo and Mexican Independence Day; battle against France; freedom from Spain; May 5; September 16; food; music; fireworks; colors of red, green; <u>Section 3:</u> Kwanzaa; lasts for a week; December; African American; celebrates community; colors of red, green, and black

New Year's Day—<u>Section 1:</u> New York City; Times Square; crystal ball; New Year's Eve; <u>Section 2:</u> Chinese New Year; January 21–February 20; special meal; children get red packets with money; dragon dances; <u>Section 3:</u> Thai New Year; Songkran; April; throw cool water on people

Lesson 3 Cultures of the World, p. 148

Ways of Life—Box 1: Africa, 50 countries, Ethiopia, language = Arabic and Somali, food = vegetables and meat, injera = flat, spongy bread; Same Circle: continents; 700 million people live there; hundreds of culture groups; different languages; different foods; Box 2: Europe, 40 countries, Spain, language = Spanish, Basque, Catalan; food = main meal in afternoon;

People of the World—Box 1: choice of country/ child will vary, but student should draw and/ or describe the different clothing and different location on the map/world; Same Circle: cultural identity; traditional clothing; children live everywhere; Box 2: choice of country/child will vary, but student should draw and/or describe the different clothing and different location on the map/world;

Expressions of Culture—Box 1: Japanese architecture, wood, nature, open; Same Circle: every culture has architecture; music; dance; they are all part of cultural identity; Box 2: Brazilian music and dance; samba music, fast rhythm, dance contests, Carnival festival

Chapter 11

Lesson 1 Workers and Consumers, p. 153

People Work Together—People Depend on Producers: Producers make products. Entrepreneurs; Oscar Weissenborn made pencils. Pencils = product. Oscar Weissenborn = producer/ entrepreneur; People Buy Things: consumers; pencils; things = products; things they want and need, like toys, food, computers, cars;

People Help Each Other—People Start Businesses: business owner; needs workers; pays a wage or income; Leticia Herrera has cleaning business; Workers: wage, income, money to buy things they need; Herrera's workers fix buildings

Lesson 2 What Resources Do Businesses Need? p. 157

Resources and Examples— Natural resources, or raw materials: wood, water, metal, rocks, spring water, milk; Human resources: people, workers, sellers, delivery people, factory workers, farmers; Capital resources: tools, buildings, machines, trucks, the factory

Lesson 3 Trading with the World, p. 161

Why Do Countries Trade with Each Other?

1. Countries get things they need from other countries.

2. Trading today is easier. Goods can travel more quickly.

3. When countries export goods, they make money.

What Goods Do Countries Trade? They trade cars, trucks, computers, tea, newsprint; allow students to include items featured on the map on page 402 as well.

Lesson 4 New Technology and Businesses, p. 165

Telephone Chart—How was the technology first used? Talking between two people. Only sound could move through phone lines, or wires. How has the technology changed? Now pictures and videos can move through phone lines. Phone lines are not even needed! Cell phones do not need phone lines. People can send all kinds of information using other machines, like fax machines and computers. How is the technology used today? How has it changed businesses? Today, people can call a company to place an order. They can call a company to get information. They can send a fax of their order. They can receive a printed receipt over the fax machine.

Computer chart—How was the technology first used? Only one person used a computer. The computer was not hooked up to anything else. How has the technology changed? Computers are now hooked up to each other, and to many other computers. Computers can "talk" to each other. Computers can get hooked up to the Internet. How is the technology used today? How has it changed businesses? Today, businesses have websites. The websites are on the Internet. Customers can go to the business's website to learn about it. They can order products from the website, too.

Chapter 12

Lesson 1 Forms of Money, p. 169

Effects: People trade things; people use money; people use checks; people use credit cards; people used shells and beads for money.

Lesson 2 Free Market Economy, p. 173

(above the pitchers of lemonade) supply; (above the people in line) demand; (above the cash box) profit; (above the iced tea stand) competition; (caption) free enterprise

Lesson 3 Earn, Spend, and Save, p. 177

Topic EARNING	Topic SPENDING	Topic SAVING	Topic BUDGETS
What I learned	What I learned	What I learned	What I learned
People earn money from jobs. There are many ways to earn money. We can learn new ways to make an income.	People spend some of their income on things they need. Families spend money on food, homes, and clothes. They spend money for fun. They spend money to help others.	People save some of their income. People save money in banks. Banks pay people interest. People also borrow money from banks. They pay interest to borrow money.	People plan how to save and spend money. Budgets tell how people earn money. They tell how people spend money. They tell how much people save.

Lesson 4 World Businesses, p. 181

Supporting Details: There are many businesses in Tokyo. Some businesses make things to use in their own country. Other businesses send things to other countries. Some businesses are cooperatives that a group of workers own.